WHAT
THE BIBLE
TEACHES
ABOUT
THE CHURCH

WHAT THE BIBLE TEACHES ABOUT

THE
CHURCH

John F. Balchin

SERIES EDITOR: G. W. KIRBY

Tyndale House Publishers, Inc. Wheaton, Illinois

Unless otherwise stated, biblical quotations are from the *Revised Standard Version* of the Bible.

Library of Congress Catalog Card Number 79-64983. ISBN 0-8423-7883-9. Copyright © 1979 by John F. Balchin. First published in Great Britain by Kingsway Publications, Ltd. Tyndale House edition published by arrangement with Kingsway Publications, Ltd. All rights reserved. First Tyndale House printing, July 1979. Printed in the United States of America.

CONTENTS

PREFACE

Far more than we ever realize we are children of our own time. We come to any subject with unconscious presuppositions which dictate the way in which we view things. However open-minded we profess to be, we are all blinkered in some way.

This is certainly true when it comes to thinking and speaking about the church, for we are all heirs to a variety of traditions which we find extremely difficult to question, even in the light of Scripture.

My aim in writing this book has been to let the Bible speak for itself on the subject, but I am painfully aware that my very approach, the questions I have asked and the conclusions I have reached, must be limited by my own small understanding of God's people.

However, I hope that what I have written may prove to be a brief introduction for those who want to know a little more, and that, in turn, it might stimulate them to further study.

JOHN F. BALCHIN

1

WHAT IS THE CHURCH?

'I'll meet you at the church.'
  'I belong to the Church of England.'
  'I've just joined the church in the High Street.'
  'My nephew has gone into the church.'
  'The church ought to do something about it!'
  In all these sentences we are using the word *church* in a different way, and not once in the way in which it was used in the New Testament. For us the church can mean a building, or a denomination, or an organization, or the ministry, or established religion, and perhaps other things too. When a word like this has such a wide range of meaning, the danger of going to the Bible and of reading our particular understanding of the term into it is a very real one. What we ought rather to do is to start with the Bible and see what the word meant there first.
  What did 'the church' mean for those first Christians? Even when they took it up and began to use it, it was a word which had already been in use for a long time. The Greek term *ekklesia* (from which we get our word 'ecclesiastical') simply meant a meeting that had been called, a summoned assembly. It was used in the earliest days of democracy in the Greek city states where every citizen had a say in public affairs. The herald used to go through the streets calling the people out together to some public place where they would debate whatever was on the agenda. The resulting assembly was the *ekklesia* (from the two Greek words meaning 'call' and 'out').
  Even in the New Testament we find it in this neutral secular sense. When Paul was at Ephesus, his opponents instigated a

riot, and the crowd rushed to their accustomed meeting place. 'Some cried one thing, some another; for the *assembly* was in confusion, and most of them did not know why they had come together' (Acts 19:32). It was, however, an unconstitutional assembly. It had not been officially summoned, and this is why the town clerk, when he finally quietened the crowd, told them, (verse 39) 'If you seek anything further, it shall be settled in the regular assembly.' 'And when he had said this, he dismissed the assembly' (verse 41). This is exactly the same word translated elsewhere as 'church'. Its basic meaning is therefore 'a meeting'.

For Greek-speaking Jews (and there were very many in the Roman world at that time) the word had other associations. When the Old Testament had been translated into Greek for their benefit, the translators had used this term (and the similar one *synagoge* or 'synagogue') for the Hebrew terms describing the assembled company of God's people, especially in their journey from Egypt to the promised land. For example Psalm 74:2 – 'Remember thy *congregation*, which thou hast gotten of old, which thou hast redeemed to be the tribe of thy heritage!' (You have both terms together in a phrase like 'the whole assembly of the congregation of Israel', Exodus 12:6.) It is in this sense that Stephen used the word in his defence ('This is he who was in the congregation in the wilderness...' Acts 7:38), and it is also found with this meaning in an Old Testament quotation ('in the midst of the congregation I will praise thee' Hebrews 2:12). This meant that when these people became Christians, and used this word for their new found fellowship, it would have had overtones of God's choice and call.

The early church

'God's people called together' might be a fair paraphrase of what the word signified to the first Jewish Christians, with the emphasis falling on *people*. At the beginning, as we shall see, there seems to have been very little in the way of organization and – as far as we can know – no buildings, and certainly no denominational structures. The church was a group of people whose lives had been touched and transformed by the gospel.

They probably avoided the other common term 'synagogue', although it means practically the same thing, for the good reason that this was the regular term for a Jewish meeting. It is used just once for a Christian assembly in the New Testament in a letter which obviously came from and went to a particularly Jewish Christian situation. James writes about the rich man who 'comes into your assembly' (James 2:2) and the word is literally 'synagogue'. In New Testament times only certain religions were legally allowed, the Jewish faith being one of them. At the beginning Christians apparently sheltered under the legal umbrella of Judaism, and it looks as though their gatherings were regarded as just another of the 'denominational' sects within Judaism, which was fairly 'multicoloured' at that time. (In Acts 6:9 we read about several different groups – the Freedmen, the Cyrenians, the Alexandrians, those of Cilicia and Asia – who apparently had their own synagogues in Jerusalem, and probably worshipped in their own way.) It soon became obvious, as many Gentiles pressed into the church without becoming Jews, that Christians were more than just another variation on the Jewish theme. It was then that persecution began to come from the Romans. In the early days it was usually stirred up by the Jews who clearly recognized that the gospel was different from their ancestral faith. We have this well illustrated for us during Paul's stay at Corinth when the local Jews accused him before the Roman proconsul, Gallio, of 'persuading men to worship God contrary to the law' (Acts 18:13). But even before Paul could speak in his defence, Gallio had dismissed the case as being 'a matter of questions about words and names and your own [Jewish] law'. Clearly, for him, Christians shared the legal privileges of Jews.

The local church

When we study the Christian use of the word 'church' a little more closely, we can be even more specific about its New

Testament content. The early Christians used it in two ways. First of all, it meant for them any group of Christians meeting together in a particular locality. Paul and Barnabas 'met with the church, and taught a large company of people' at Antioch (Acts 11:26). On their missionary journey they 'appointed elders for them in every church' (Acts 14:23). Paul could write 'to the church of God which is at Corinth' (1 Corinthians 1:2), 'to the church of the Thessalonians' (1 Thessalonians 1:1) and so on. It was in this sense of the word that he could also talk about 'the churches of God' (1 Corinthians 11:16), that is, the various groups of Christians meeting in different places, but each deserving the description 'church' or 'assembly'.

Many of these gatherings were small enough to meet in homes. Prisca and Aquila had a church in their house in Rome (Romans 16:5), while a group at Laodicea met in the home of a lady called Nympha (Colossians 4:15). Before there were buildings set aside for the purpose, it was most natural to take advantage of the hospitality of one of the members and to meet at his or her house. We find some of the Christians at Jerusalem gathered together and praying for the imprisoned Peter at Mary's house (Acts 12:12) and there must have been many other house groups like that one in the city at the time. As far as we can see, they only met together when they went up together to worship in the Temple. 'They were all together in Solomon's Portico,' (Acts 5:12), which was probably in one of the outer courtyards where there was room for the crowd. It was in the Temple that the apostles taught the fellowship (Acts 5:21), although they held the more intimate service of communion in their homes (Acts 2:46).

Although fellowship was very close in such domestic surroundings, we must not take all this to mean that Christian groups *must* meet in homes in order to be churches. The purpose was entirely practical. It was simply a matter of keeping the rain off! We know that on one occasion Paul seems to have taken a hall (the one belonging to Tyrannus at Ephesus, Acts 19:9) no doubt in order to get everyone in who wanted to listen to him.

The universal church

The other use of the word 'church' is what we can only call a 'universal' sense, that is, of all God's people everywhere. Paul writes of Christ as being 'the head over all things for the church, which is his body, the fulness of him who fills all in all' (Ephesians 1:22f.). It is in 'the church' (not 'the churches') that we see God's great purpose working out (Ephesians 3:10). He can describe his sufferings as being 'for the sake of his (Christ's) body, that is, the church' (Colossians 1:24). In these verses and others the whole company of the redeemed are seen as one unit.

These two uses of the word 'church', the local and the universal, are not exclusive or contradictory. The church at large outcrops in particular localities. Each local group represents the universal community. This means that in New Testament terms, the smallest group of believers is just as much God's church as the largest.

Jesus and the church

It is interesting that Jesus only used the word twice in his recorded teaching, and that when he did, it was in these two senses of local and universal. When Peter first confessed Christ in a perceptive way, Jesus replied with the famous play on words, 'You are Peter, [which means 'rock'] and on this rock I will build my church, and the gates of Hades shall not prevail against it.' (Matthew 16:18–19.) Endless discussion has centred on the precise meaning of 'this rock'. For the Roman Catholics it has been the Scripture prop for the authority of the Pope. They have argued that Christ appointed Peter as his supreme delegate on earth, and that Peter's successors have the same authority passed on to them. Moreover, they maintain that Peter was the first bishop of Rome, something very difficult to establish from a historical point of view, and that therefore the bishop of Rome, or the Pope, must be the chief executive of the church.

Protestants have usually replied that this is far from Christ's intention in these words. They have pointed out that Paul could categorically state that 'no other foundation can any one lay than that which is laid, which is Jesus Christ,' (1 Corinthians 3:11), so that what is in question here is not so much Peter as his faith in Christ. This formed the starting point of the church Christ has in mind. The idea of Christ as a rock or a stone comes elsewhere in the New Testament. Peter himself claimed before the Jewish council 'this is the stone which was rejected by you builders, but which has become the head of the corner.' (Acts 4:11 alluding to the words in Psalm 118:22.) When he wrote his first letter he took a similar line (1 Peter 2:6–8):

> It stands in scripture: 'Behold, I am laying in Zion a stone, a cornerstone chosen and precious, and he who believes in him will not be put to shame.' To you therefore who believe, he is precious, but for those who do not believe, 'The very stone which the builders rejected has become the head of the corner,' and 'A stone that will make men stumble, a rock that will make them fall' ...

Paul seems to get the best of both ideas when he describes the church as 'built upon the foundation of the apostles and prophets, Christ Jesus himself being the cornerstone' (Ephesians 2:20).

The image that Jesus used was one of a city well founded on an unshakable rock foundation. It stands in opposition to another city, Hades, which was the Greek name for the place of the dead. The meaning of Christ's words is that even death cannot hold back those who are true citizens in Christ's church. Human organizations need continual replenishment or continually grow smaller simply because death takes its toll. The church can never grow smaller. When Christians die we may take their names off earthly church rolls, but they never cease to be members of Christ's church; (which, of course, is no reason for leaving them on our church rolls which are simply an indication of who is identified with a particular local group at one time). Traditionally, those still with us have been called 'the church militant', that is, still fighting a spiritual battle in a hostile world, while those who have gone on have been called 'the church triumphant', enjoying rest in Christ's presence. Let us remember, however, that although our circumstances may be very different, our status in God's sight is exactly the same.

On the other occasion that Jesus used the word 'church' it has to do with disputes between individual disciples. If all else fails, they were to 'tell it to the church' (Matthew 18:17). Jesus is obviously not talking about the universal church this time, but rather the local group and its responsibility to sort out its own quarrels and differences. It is significant that it is in this context that we have the famous text 'For where two or three are gathered in my name, there am I in the midst of them,' (Matthew 18:20), which is probably the simplest statement of what 'church' means in the New Testament.

In New Testament terms then, 'church' means a group of people who find themselves in a new relationship with one another because of their new relationship with Christ. This was no mistaken development, as some have suggested. It was clearly part of Christ's purpose for his disciples. In fact, from a biblical point of view, it might be more accurate to say that Christ came, died and rose again in order to save a people for himself, that is, for his very own, rather than to concentrate on individual believers as we often do. In the New Testament we find that Christians were saved together and not just as isolated units. The result of the preaching of the gospel was not just individual believers; it was the church, the New Covenant people of God.

2

GOD DEALS WITH GROUPS

One of the criticisms levelled against Evangelical Christians in recent years is that they have had no doctrine of the church, and there is some truth in this. We have stressed the need for the individual to come to faith in Christ, spoken of individual discipleship and individual holiness for so long that we have often forgotten that, in Scripture, God dealt with groups as well as with individuals.

God and the community

God sees the whole human race as one unit. All are, to use Paul's words, 'in Adam' (1 Corinthians 15:22), and express that solidarity, that 'belonging together', by sharing a common fallen human nature and a common fate. 'God so loved *the world* . . .' as well as individuals. He is 'the Saviour of *all* men, especially of those who believe,' (1 Timothy 4:10) and it could be fairly said that the New Testament describes God's people as a new humanity, recreated in Christ and made one by his Spirit. This is what Paul meant when he told the Ephesians that Christ 'is our peace', breaking down 'the dividing wall of hostility' . . . 'that he might create in himself one new man in place of the two, so making peace' (Ephesians 2:14–16). Even the deep gulf between Jew and non-Jew had been bridged.

Christ is regarded by Paul as being the last Adam, summing up a new race just as the first Adam did (1 Corinthians 15:45). His purpose is nothing less than the remaking of mankind in its original design. The new, Christian nature is 'being renewed in knowledge after the image of its creator. Here there cannot be Greek and Jew, circumcised and uncircumcised, barbarian, Scythian, slave, free man, but Christ is all, and in all.' (Colossians 3:10–11.) Man was originally in God's image before he fell (Genesis 1:26–27), and the Christian gospel involves re-creation in that image. However, it is more than just individual transformation. Man was made to live in community, and so the church should express something of the restoration of that community of men and women here on earth. Certainly in its final form the church was seen by John to be truly international in composition. God had taken people 'from every tribe and tongue and people and nation' and 'made them a kingdom and priests' (Revelation 5:9–10).

However, long before the Christian church came on the scene, God began to work out his saving purpose through groups. Abraham was called not simply for his own sake, but for the sake of the nation which would spring from him and which, in turn, would become a blessing to all the families of the earth (Genesis 12:2). God promised a man who was childless at that time that his descendants would be more numerous than the stars of heaven (Genesis 15:1–5), that he would become the father of a multitude of nations (Genesis 17:1–8), and that by his descendants 'all the nations of the earth' would 'bless themselves' (Genesis 22:18). These promises followed his line, passing to Isaac (Genesis 26:1–5) and to the unlikely Jacob (Genesis 28:13f.) whose name God changed to Israel (Genesis 35:9f.). His sons and their descendants became 'the children of Israel' and the subject of special promises and dealings. 'I will take you for my people, and I will be your God,' said the Lord (Exodus 6:7).

It was as an embryo nation that God brought them out of the slavery of Egypt and made a special agreement, or covenant, with them, pledging himself to them, and binding them in service to him. It was not because they deserved it or that they had anything to commend themselves by. 'It was not because you were more in number than any other people that the LORD set his love upon you and chose you, for you were the fewest of all peoples; but it is because the LORD loves you, and is keeping the oath which he swore to your fathers...' (Deuteronomy 7:7–8).

Later leaders of Israel would come to found their hope for the nation on this fact that Israel belonged in a special way to God himself. 'Thou didst establish for thyself thy people Israel,' says king David, 'to be thy people for ever; and thou, O LORD, didst become their God' (2 Samuel 7:24). This became particularly so when the people sinned and when God judged them as a nation by allowing the over-running of their territory by their enemies, and ultimately by arranging their exile from the land they loved. It was as a group that he brought some of them back, although many scattered among the nations and have remained there until the present day. The extraordinary thing is that Israel's descendants are *still* a recognizable entity, even after two thousand years of living within non-Jewish society and, until recently, without a land of their own.

It was in the ruins of the Old Covenant that God gave his servants the vision of a new arrangement on a somewhat different basis, a New Covenant unlike the Old. It would include a new basis for godly living. God would put his law within them and write it upon their hearts. It would be associated with forgiveness of sins, and the old promise would be updated: 'I will be their God, and they shall be my people.' (Jeremiah 31:31–34.) As we shall see, however, the blessings would spill over beyond the borders of the natural Israel to the other families and nations included in the original promises.

When Christ began his ministry one of the first things he did was to form a group who were personally committed to him. This very number, twelve, seems to indicate that they were to represent the twelve tribes that had failed. (On one occasion Jesus promised that they would 'sit on twelve thrones, judging the twelve tribes of Israel' Matthew 19:28; Luke 22:30.) As such the disciples stood in a prophetic tradition which went right back to the time of Elijah. He thought that he was the only one left who was faithful to the Lord, but God had to inform him that there was still a group, 'seven thousand in Israel

... that have not bowed to Baal' (1 Kings 19:18). This idea of a faithful few became known as 'the remnant', and we find it strongly emphasized in the later prophets. When the rest of the nation was backslidden, God always preserved some who were still wholly committed to him. Here we have the beginnings of the idea of a 'spiritual' Israel, that is, that God's true people are not just the physical descendants of Abraham, Isaac and Jacob, but their spiritual heirs. The Jews of Jesus' time relied heavily on their physical descent. 'Abraham is our father,' they told him (John 8:39). That is why they were upset by John the Baptist. 'Do not presume to say to yourselves, "We have Abraham as our father";' he said, 'for I tell you, God is able from these stones to raise up children to Abraham.' (Matthew 3:9.) Jesus told them that uncomfortable story about the unjust tenants of the vineyard who, instead of paying the rent, maltreated the owner's servants and killed his son. The owner would quite rightly come and punish them 'and let out the vineyard to other tenants who will give him the fruits of their season' (Matthew 21:33–46). No wonder the chief priests and the Pharisees 'perceived that he was speaking about them'. The vine and the vineyard were regular Old Testament pictures of Israel, of God's people.

As we have seen, Jesus' use of the word 'church' makes it clear that he intended to found a community. The Lord's Supper is a community meal. The command to baptize and teach (Matthew 28:19) involves the extension of the community. Some have argued that the church was never Jesus' intention and that it grew out of an early misunderstanding of his teaching. We can only come to that conclusion if we are prepared to edit his words. Others have argued from what is known as the 'Dispensationalist' point of view that Christ should have been received and hailed as King by the Jews when he first came. When this did not happen, the church came into being as an interim measure until the postponed Jewish kingdom comes at the end. Without prejudging the issue of Israel's future, this view appears to make the church an afterthought. The New Testament makes it central to God's purpose in the world.

The scope of the church

Jesus' teaching about the kingdom of God (or 'kingdom of heaven', which is just a different way of saying the same thing) has a community aspect. The Jews had been expecting a king and a kingdom for years. The Old Testament prophecies assured them that both would come in God's good time. However, over against the popular view of the Jews of his day who expected a purely earthly reign and ruler, Jesus preached the kingdom as the dynamic rule of God breaking into the world, and especially into the lives of those who received the gospel message. (In fact, the earliest Christian missionaries also preached 'the kingdom', not 'the church': e.g. Acts 8:12; 19:8; 20:25.) It would be wrong to identify the church with the kingdom as the latter is a much bigger concept, although the kingdom creates the church and the church represents the kingdom. Perhaps 'the kingdom in the making' expresses something of their relationship to one another.

There are some who would make the church inclusive of all whom God has chosen and called from the very beginning, right back to Seth, in fact (Genesis 4:25). Others have dated the church's birthday as either the occasion of Jesus' calling of the Twelve, or at least of Peter's confession of faith at Caesarea Philippi (Matthew 16:13–20). Some have felt that it is the post-resurrection community which was commissioned to spread the gospel which really deserves the title 'church' (Luke 24:36–49). Whereas there is some truth in all these views, it is most generally held that in the more limited sense of 'the Christian church' we must go to Pentecost (Acts 2), which marks the dividing line between the ministry of Christ and the new and enlarged ministry of the Holy Spirit. God dealt with them as a group in a new way, and those who responded to their Spirit-filled evangelism were 'added' to that group Acts (2:41). Perhaps even more significantly, we come across the word 'fellowship' for the first time (Acts 2:42). All had individually responded to the call to repentance, and all had been baptized in the name of Jesus Christ for the forgiveness of their sins. All had received the gift of the Holy Spirit (Acts 2:38). In so doing they discovered a new oneness, not only with God in Christ, but also with others with whom they had previously had little in common. God himself had given them a whole new basis for belonging together, a New Covenant which was no respecter of persons. However the Lord had dealt with different groupings in the past here there could not be any distinction between Jews and Gentiles, slaves or free men: Christ was 'all and in all' (Colossians 3:11).

It is in this sense that the church deserves the title 'catholic', which means 'universal'. Roman Catholics have traditionally claimed the term for themselves because of their worldwide agreement in matters of belief and practice. True catholicity, however, goes back to Christ's words in the great commission, 'Go, make disciples of *all nations...*' (Matthew 28:19), and they did, although they came to the practical implications slowly. Peter had to learn that 'God shows no partiality, but in every nation any one who fears him and does what is right is acceptable to him' (Acts 10:34f.).

A similar term is 'ecumenical' which derives from the Greek word meaning 'the whole inhabited world'. Jesus said that 'this gospel of the kingdom will be preached throughout the whole [inhabited] world, as a testimony to all nations' (Matthew 24:14). His concern was for the worldwide spread of the good news, and in that the church continues to preach 'to every creature under heaven' (Colossians 1:23) it may claim the description.

3

THE NEW SHARING

Fellowship

Like the other terms adopted by first century Christians, 'fellowship' had been widely used previously in secular ways. The word comes from a fairly common root meaning 'to share' or 'to have in common'. It signified 'to participate in something' rather than 'to share out something to others', though the one often issued in the other. In the Greek world it had been used of business partnerships, of friendships, of marriage and, in pagan worship, of the intimate relationship which the worshipper claimed to have with his god. We have this latter use illustrated for us in one of the problems at Corinth. The Christians there thought nothing of going to eat a sacrificial meal in a pagan temple, something which was a regular social occasion in those days. Paul points out that eating in this way was part of pagan worship and, in fact, expressed a fellowship that they ought to avoid at all costs, for behind the idols stood demonic forces utterly opposed to Christ and to the gospel (1 Corinthians 10:14–22).

Strange to say that although the word 'fellowship' was used in the Greek version of the Old Testament, it was never used by the Jews of their relationship with God, only with other people. The nearest we ever get to the New Testament idea is the close circle of disciples around their rabbi or teacher, an allegiance also expressed by eating together.

The early Christians discovered that, despite their international roots, they had a great deal in common: a 'common faith' and a 'common salvation' (Titus 1:4; Jude 3). The gospel transformed the word 'fellowship' for believers. By the indwelling Spirit they had been brought into the closest of relationships with Christ. God had 'called [them] into the fellowship of his Son' (1 Corinthians 1:9). In Paul's language, they found themselves 'in Christ', identified with him and his work, incorporated into his body, the church. The effect of their new oneness with Christ was a new link with every other believer who had been 'born again'. Fellowship is two-way: with the Lord and, as a result, with one another. 'That which we have seen and heard we proclaim also to you, so that you may have fellowship with us;' wrote John, 'and our fellowship is with the Father and with his Son Jesus Christ.' (1 John 1:3.) To claim fellowship with God means that we must 'walk in the light' and then we shall have 'fellowship with one another' (1 John 1:7).

It is not simply a matter of sharing the same opinions about God or the gospel. Converted people share the same Spirit. When Paul wished for his Corinthian friends 'the grace of our Lord Jesus Christ and the love of God and *the fellowship of the Holy Spirit*' (2 Corinthians 13:14), he was not speaking so much about fellowship *with* the Holy Spirit as about sharing in, participating in the Holy Spirit. He uses the same ground as an appeal for unity in the church at Philippi: 'If there is any encouragement in Christ, any incentive of love, any participation in the Spirit...' (Philippians 2:1), Christ had consoled them. His love was the incentive to them to love others, but they also shared the same Spirit, that is, they shared the same divine life as the branches share the sap of the same tree, a picture which Paul uses for Gentiles and Jews in fellowship (Romans 11:17–18).

The grounds of this fellowship are therefore inherent in genuine Christian experience. To be one with other believers was a direct result of their conversion. It was not merely a matter of people co-operating because they had a common interest like photography or fishing. There was a supernatural basis for their new found relationships with one another. Hence Paul exhorts

them to '*maintain* the unity of the Spirit' (Ephesians 4:3), not
to make it. If their experience of Christ by the Spirit was real,
then they already possessed it. It was created by the Spirit and
as we have seen, emerges in the New Testament record for the
first time at Pentecost. There those who received the message,
after being baptized, 'devoted themselves to the apostles' teaching and *fellowship*, to the breaking of bread and the prayers'
(Acts 2:42).

This new sharing expressed itself in a number of ways. There
was, first of all, a sense of belonging in those early churches
which cut across all other natural barriers. Men and women
previously divided by race, culture, religion, sex, social status
or even language now addressed each other as 'brother' or
'sister', and these were not empty titles. The Spirit was the
Spirit of adoption, and therefore they were members of the same
family, of 'the household of God' (Ephesians 2:19; 1 Timothy
3:15; Galatians 6:10). The young Timothy was told by Paul
to conduct himself within the church fellowship as he would
within a family situation: 'Do not rebuke an older man but
exhort him as you would a father; treat younger men like
brothers, older women like mothers, younger women like sisters,
in all purity.' (1 Timothy 5:1f.) At times it meant radical changes
in existing relationships. Because Onesimus had been converted,
his master Philemon had to receive back his runaway slave 'no
longer as a slave but more than a slave, as a beloved brother'
(Philemon 16). True, this came hard to some who still wanted
to retain the old distinctions of status. James takes such to
task because they were distinguishing between the rich and the
poor (James 2:1–4), but then he could only do so because they
were brethren in Christ.

Sharing means also making your contribution to the whole,
and this at a spiritual level. All had something to offer in terms
of mutual ministry expressed in the oft repeated phrase 'one
another'. They were to 'love one another' (Romans 13:8) and
therefore they were not to pass judgement on one another
(Romans 14:13). They were to welcome one another (Romans
15:7) whilst not provoking or envying one another (Galatians

5:26). They were to bear one another's burdens (Galatians 6:2), be kind to one another, forgiving one another (Ephesians 4:32), comforting, encouraging, building one another up (1 Thessalonians 4:18; 5:11). The reason that Paul gives for such practical action was that they were 'members one of another', limbs sharing the same body life (Ephesians 4:25). Although the New Testament writers found it necessary to remind their friends about this mutual ministry, it was something which, in the last analysis, they could only learn from God, which many apparently did quite spontaneously. Paul records that the Thessalonians had no need to have anything written to them about 'love of the brethren', 'for you yourselves have been taught by God to love one another' (1 Thessalonians 4:9). They had learned to share and to minister to one another. Even a man like the apostle who undoubtedly had an exceptional ministry and a great deal to offer still expected to benefit from the experience of others. He longed to see the Christians in Rome, not only because he wanted to preach and teach there, but also, he says, 'that we may be mutually encouraged by each other's faith, both yours and mine' (Romans 1:12).

Material sharing

Their concern, however, was much more than just a 'spiritual' one. This new sharing expressed itself in intensely practical ways. One of the spontaneous results of Pentecost was that 'all who believed were together and had all things in common; and they sold their possessions and goods, and distributed them to all, as any had need' (Acts 2:44f.). There is no evidence that this early experiment of living from a common fund was ever repeated, although there is plenty that Christians cared for one another in practical and material ways. 'Do not neglect to do good,' we read, 'and to share what you have, for such sacrifices are pleasing to God.' (Hebrews 13:16.) Some were naturally better qualified to do this than others and therefore had a special ministry in this direction. Some could prophesy, some could teach, but equally some could give, and they were exhorted to

do so liberally (Romans 12:8). In fact, this was one way for
the rich man to guarantee that his wealth did not distract him
from his trust in Christ. 'They are to do good,' says Paul, 'to
be rich in good deeds, liberal and generous, thus laying up for
themselves a good foundation for the future.' (1 Timothy
6:17–18.)

Some went on record for their particularly generous hospitality, entertaining Christians passing through their town, and
as we have seen, sometimes opening their homes to the whole
church for somewhere to meet. Gaius was host to Paul 'and
to the whole church' (Romans 16:23), while the apostle could
confidently ask Philemon, 'prepare a guest room for me'
(Philemon 22).

At Ephesus there was special care shown to widows who
had no other means of support, although Paul is careful to
instruct Timothy not to be taken in by the frivolous, or the
young and active, or by those who had children or relatives
who should have been supporting them (1 Timothy 5:3–16).
It looks as though the New Testament church had its quota
of spongers too, and the Thessalonian letters deal quite firmly
with such (1 Thessalonians 5:14; 2 Thessalonians 3:6–13).

This material sharing also took place between local churches.
The Jerusalem Christians, for example, knew what poverty was
all about. Very early on we find Paul and Barnabas taking a
gift to them from the church at Antioch in time of famine
(Acts 11:27–30). When Paul's mission among the Gentiles had
progressed, and had produced healthy and, one assumes,
wealthy churches, he conceived the idea of taking up a collection
for them once again. We have, therefore, a protracted appeal
for such gifts when he wrote to the Corinthians (2 Corinthians
8–9). This was to be a practical expression of sharing.

> I do not mean that others should be eased and you burdened, but
> that as a matter of equality your abundance at the present time
> should supply their want, so that their abundance may supply
> your want, that there may be equality. (2 Corinthians 8:13f.)

It was to be completely voluntary, simply something in return for the spiritual blessings which had come to them from the 'home base' of the gospel. 'If the Gentiles have come to share in their spiritual blessings,' he argues, 'they ought also to be of service to them in material blessings.' (Romans 15:27, where the word 'fellowship' is actually used for their contribution.) Christian love had to be practical to be genuine. 'If any one has the world's goods and sees his brother in need, yet closes his heart against him, how does God's love abide in him?' asks John (1 John 3:17).

The same principle could also operate at a personal level between the church and the Christian worker serving the church. Paul makes it quite clear that such deserve support, even though he himself had refused it: 'the Lord commanded that those who proclaim the gospel should get their living by the gospel.' (1 Corinthians 9:14.) It was again a two-way sharing. The worker shared spiritual things with the church; the church shared its material blessings with the worker. 'If we have sown spiritual good among you, is it too much if we reap your material benefits?' (1 Corinthians 9:11.) Paul, in an effort to put no obstacles in the way of his ministry, never expected such support. The only church which broke this rule for him illustrates the principle. The Philippian Christians had sent him gifts more than once, just as he had ministered to their spiritual needs (Philippians 4:10–20). Yet this was not just a financial arrangement, it was a 'partnership [or fellowship] . . . of giving and receiving', an intensely practical way of sharing.

Belonging, sharing, caring . . . and suffering: these were the things that the early believers had in common, and probably because of the last in the list knew themselves to be much closer to one another than we are today. Paul described those same Philippian Christians as suffering for the sake of Christ, 'engaged in the same conflict which you saw and now hear to be mine' (Philippians 1:29–30). The apostle reckoned that such suffering for the truth and for the sake of the church was in some ways participation in the very suffering of Christ. 'We share abundantly in Christ's sufferings,' he wrote (2 Corinthians 1:5). 'I rejoice in my sufferings for your sake, and in my flesh

I complete what is lacking in Christ's afflictions for the sake of his body, that is, the church.' (Colossians 1:24). It was as though Christ himself suffered in the sufferings of his people.

Evangelical concern

One last aspect of fellowship hardly needs describing. They shared a common concern that the gospel might be made known to others as yet outside the bounds of their own partnership. Paul thanks God for the Philippians' 'partnership [or fellowship] in the gospel from the first day until now' (Philippians 1:5). They were all, he said, 'partakers with me of grace, both in my imprisonment and in the defence and confirmation of the gospel' (Philippians 1:7). Apostles like Paul expected and rejoiced in the backing of the churches as they made Christ known. Just as 'fellowship' had once been used for business associations, they found themselves in business together, labouring side by side in the preaching of the gospel (Philippians 4:3). The whole church together was the representative of Christ in the world, and in this way they saw the practical fulfilment of Christ's words to his Father (John 17:22f.):

> The glory which thou hast given me I have given to them, that they may be one even as we are one, I in them and thou in me, that they may become perfectly one, so that the world may know that thou hast sent me. . . .

4

THE BODY OF CHRIST

One of the best known New Testament descriptions of the church is 'the body of Christ'. Actually it is only used by the apostle Paul, but it well sums up the ideas of unity and diversity among God's people.

The body and its head

There may be something of a development in Paul's use of this striking picture. When he uses it first in Romans and 1 Corinthians, (Romans 12:3–8; 1 Corinthians 12:12–31) it is in order to illustrate the place of differently gifted Christians within the life of the whole. No particular place is given to the head. It is simply mentioned in passing: 'The eye cannot say to the hand, "I have no need of you," nor again the head to the feet, "I have no need of you."' (1 Corinthians 12:21.) Later on in Colossians and Ephesians the church is the body, and Christ is distinctly the head: 'he has made him the head over all things for the church, which is his body,' (Ephesians 1:22–23). 'He is the head of the body, the church.' (Colossians 1:18.)

There is no need to assume, as some have, that Paul got a completely different idea from somewhere for his later references. The themes are already present elsewhere in his earlier writings. For example, he describes Christ as 'the head of every man' (1 Corinthians 11:3) in the marriage relationship, an idea that he develops later in Ephesians when he illustrates the same theme by speaking of Christ's love for his church. 'The husband is the head of the wife as Christ is the head of the church, his

body, and is himself its Saviour.' (See Ephesians 5:21–33.) God
the Holy Spirit fused the ideas together in Paul's mind to give
us an image which has become proverbial of the church and
its 'members' or limbs.

'The body of Christ' has suggested to some more than just
an illustration. They have argued that it tells us something
important about Christ himself. A head does not exist on its
own. It *needs* a body to complete it. So, some have claimed,
Christ *needs* his church; in fact, he is incomplete without it.
Some would understand Paul to be saying this when he says
that 'the church is the completion of Christ who (as the church
grows) will be totally completed' (Ephesians 1:23 their translation). This idea has been employed particularly by those who
have a very elevated view of the church and its authority. One
high church bishop once said that 'the church is the extension
and the perpetuation of the Incarnation in the world', which
means, of course, that we should expect the church to
speak, through its leaders, with the authority of Christ. For
others, however, to say that Christ is incomplete does less
than justice to the eternal Son of God, and to speak of the
church as his completion seems to give undue dignity to the
church.

The real question is whether or not Paul's words can really
bear this meaning, and when we examine them we find that
the apostle does not appear to be as exact in his descriptions
as this. For example, Christ is also described as 'the head
of all rule and authority' (Colossians 2:10), although there
is no suggestion that 'all rule and authority' is his body as
well. As we have seen, the idea of the head also appears in
the husband/bride picture (Ephesians 5:23, 28–30). It might
therefore be better to understand the head and body image
as just one picture among many that Paul uses for the church.
He can also speak of it as the new Israel, the bride, the
temple, the new humanity and so on, all of which emphasize
important aspects of the church's character and life.

There are certainly several fundamental truths tied up in
the idea of the church as Christ's body. Not the least is that

of our 'solidarity', our 'belonging together', as Christians who share the same life, the same privileges and the same responsibilities. This idea comes across frequently in the Old Testament. For example, a man was the head of his family and involved his own in all that he did (e.g. Joshua 7 where Achan broke God's law in the storming of Jericho and brought judgement on his whole family). In a similar way the king was the head of the nation and represented the nation where God was concerned. As we have already seen, in the Old Testament God dealt with and judged his people as a group, a fact of which Paul reminds the Corinthians when they were tempted to sit back and rely on their privileges (1 Corinthians 10:1–13). Perhaps the strongest parallel is the one we have already noted between Adam and Christ. We are 'in Adam' by birth; we are 'in Christ' by faith and the operation of the Holy Spirit, and this, for Paul, is much more than just an individual affair. To be 'in Christ' is almost the same as saying 'in the body'. The Messiah and his people are one, and that in the closest possible sense. The body is a picture of what we might call an organic rather than just an organized togetherness. Limbs cannot live by themselves and they are not merely arranged together. They need to be organically linked to one another and they need the same head. They must share the same life.

Jesus had already taught this 'organic' oneness between himself and his disciples, although with the use of a different picture, that of the vine. He claimed to be 'the true vine', probably in contrast to the Jewish nation of which the vine was a symbol. His disciples were like branches but could only hope to bear fruit and fulfil their purpose if they continued to 'abide' in him, that is, remain organically attached to him so that his life might flow into theirs (John 15:1–11). Paul is teaching the same truth but using the picture of head and body.

Actually he begins 'at the other end' from where we normally would. We tend to begin to think about the church as a group which then has to discover and work out its oneness. Paul begins with the oneness of the body which then goes on to discover its diversity.

We must be careful in handling this picture not to turn the clock back and read modern medical understanding into the New Testament. As far as we know, it was not common knowledge in the first century that the function of the brain was to direct the body. We have only come to know that since. Paul is using the word 'head' against a different background, although coming up with similar ideas. In the Old Testament, in which Paul would have been steeped as a Jew, the head means either 'chief' or 'beginning'. Because of Christ's triumph on the cross, he is 'head over all things' (Ephesians 1:22), 'of all rule and authority' (Colossians 2:10), that is, he wields authority over all creation. All authority has been given to him in heaven and on earth (Matthew 28:18).

Christians, who acknowledge Christ's lordship in their lives, actively share in that glorious triumph in a conscious way. They anticipate the great Day when 'every knee should bow ... and every tongue confess that Jesus Christ is Lord' (Philippians 2:10f.). But collectively Christ is also Lord and as such he guides and directs his people in their affairs. Understood in terms of the local fellowship of believers, this means that the church can expect Christ as head to lead his own directly, a fact strongly emphasized in some forms of church government where the local fellowship is regarded as responsible to Christ alone and not to some denominational structure.

Christ, however, not only directs the obedient church, he is also the source of its life.

We are to grow up in every way into him who is the head, into Christ, *from whom* the whole body, joined and knit together by every joint with which it is supplied, when each part is working properly, makes bodily growth and upbuilds itself in love. (Ephesians 4:15f.)

It is Christ who 'nourishes and cherishes' the church, 'because we are members of his body' (Ephesians 5:29f.). Our unity with one another derives from our oneness with him who is the head. Seen negatively, the false teachers at Colossae were divisive simply because they did not 'hold fast to the head' (see Colossians 2:19).

The body and its members

Paul also places stress on the way in which individual limbs relate to one another. His original motive in using the picture was to settle differences within a church where some obviously thought that they were superior to others (1 Corinthians 12:12–31). He insists that each individual's spiritual endowment comes from the one Spirit, and that our differences are like the different functions of individual limbs within the body. None do exactly the same job, but all are mutually interdependent for the proper functioning of the whole. He asks what would happen if the limbs started asserting their independence and telling the rest that they did not need them. As it is they – and we – all need one another.

This lays the responsibility for maintaining the harmonious working of the fellowship on each individual member. They must recognize that *all* gifts come from God, and that *all* have some necessary function to fulfil. Each part must work properly, and that means that each Christian must recognize and exercise the gift God has granted him or her, while neither envying nor despising others whose contribution might be different. 'Having gifts that differ according to the grace given to us, let us use them,' Paul writes (Romans 12:6).

The difference between any ordinary group of people and the church, however, is that in the latter case the differences are not just accidental. They are ordained by God and part of his way of fulfilling his will in and through the church, together with the fact that our very being together is a supernatural thing. We are actually related to one another and to the head by the Holy Spirit.

5

UNITY – AND DIVISION

In New Testament terms, the church is one. Jesus prayed for his disciples in the upper room that they might be one in the same way that he was one with the Father (John 17:20–21), and that included those who would come to faith in him through their witness. If we want to know what unity means, therefore, we must think of Father and Son, and of the love that flowed between them. Christ's 'new commandment' to his disciples was 'that you love one another; even as I have loved you,' (John 13:34), and this as we have seen was the concern of the apostolic writers.

Christian unity

Paul describes spiritual unity in a sevenfold way. It is as though we have seven things in common (Ephesians 4:4–6). There is 'one body' of which all Christians were limbs or members. There is 'one Spirit' in whom they all shared and who indwelt each one. They had been called to 'one hope', that is, they had a common destiny and heritage. They were all going the same way. There is 'one Lord' to whom they all owed allegiance, and who owned them just as surely as masters did their slaves. There is 'one faith': they had been converted when they had accepted the terms of a common gospel. There is 'one baptism', initially expressing and confessing that faith. There is 'one God' who is Father to all he has adopted into his family.

There are also distinctions and divisions in the church,

some legitimate, some not so. Paul goes on in this same passage, for example, to point out that this oneness does not mean that we all make the same contribution to the life of the whole. 'Grace was given to each of us according to the measure of Christ's gift.' (Ephesians 4:7.) Equal in status, we are different in function and all have distinct ministries. Such distinctions are God-given. There are, however, some which are not.

Divisive issues

It should go without saying that there were no denominations in the modern sense of the the word in New Testament times. The denominational divisions which cut clean across the modern churches are part of our unfortunate heritage from the history of the church since then. But we should not jump to the conclusion that the New Testament churches were perfect in respect to their ideal oneness, or in any other way. The churches we read about were beset by many deep problems. Had it not been so, we would not have had much of the New Testament as we now have it. A good number of the letters were written to meet problems in the churches with which some of our present day difficulties seem mild by comparison.

There were many divisive issues which broke up the ideal unity of which we have been speaking. Sometimes it was simply personal disagreement which spoiled the harmony. New Testament Christians were real people with human natures like our own, not plaster saints. In a particularly frank passage (Acts 15:36–41) we find even Paul and Barnabas painted 'warts and all', falling out over whether or not Mark should join them on their second missionary journey. In the event they could only agree to go their separate ways. 'There arose a sharp contention, so that they separated from each other; Barnabas took Mark with him and sailed away to Cyprus, but Paul chose Silas and departed....' We know that the quarrel was resolved later, because we find Paul

recommending the same Mark (Colossians 4:10) and request-
ing that he join him again because he had been very useful
in serving him (2 Timothy 4:11). Some have argued that,
had there been no quarrel, Cyprus would not have been
visited again, but although God certainly over-rules our
mistakes, this kind of division between respected Christian
workers must always be tragic.

It must have been a similar personal upset, probably too
trivial to mention in detail, which kept the two ladies at
Philippi, Euodia and Syntyche, at loggerheads with one
another (Philippians 4:2). Paul first of all tackles the problem
obliquely, not mentioning them individually, but rather spelling out how Christians ought to live worthily of the gospel.
This involves standing 'firm in one spirit, with one mind
striving side by side for the faith of the gospel' (Philippians
1:27). He then goes on to list the reasons for being at one
with other Christians, even appealing to the example of Christ
as a pattern for our humility which is the key to accepting
others (Philippians 2:1–11), 'Do nothing from selfishness or
conceit,' he says (verse 3), 'but in humility count others better
than yourselves.' Only later in the letter does he speak to
them directly, appealing to a friend to try and bring them
together again (4:2–3).

It is at Corinth that we have the nearest to 'denominational'
differences that we can find in the New Testament. The
church had been exposed to a succession of different teachers,
and members were lining up behind them and setting them
off against one another. Each one was saying, 'I belong to
Paul' or 'I belong to Apollos' or 'I belong to Cephas' or 'I
belong to Christ' (1 Corinthians 1:12). Under God, Paul had
founded the church, and as he pointed out, he was not too
concerned with rhetorical eloquence or intellectual sophisti-
cation. 'I did not come to you,' he says, 'proclaiming to you
the testimony of God in lofty words or wisdom. For I decided
to know nothing among you except Jesus Christ and him
crucified.' (1 Corinthians 2:1f.) His one aim was to see men
and women confronted with the message of the cross,

although it might not be very flattering and certainly would not satisfy the worldly-wise. However, that was part of the policy. He wanted genuine conversions, not merely intellectual adherence. What God had done at Corinth he had done by his own power and not by Paul's cleverness (1 Corinthians 2:3–5).

After Paul left, a very different kind of preacher came to Corinth. His name was Apollos, and we know something of his background from the book of Acts. He came from Alexandria, a university city in those days, and 'he was an eloquent man, well versed in the scriptures' (Acts 18:24). We also know that he was a very humble man who was prepared to learn from Priscilla and Aquila and make up what was deficient in his understanding of Christian things. He gained quite a reputation as a preacher in Ephesus and was encouraged to go across to Greece and minister there. 'When he arrived, he greatly helped those who through grace had believed, for he powerfully confuted the Jews in public, showing by the scriptures that the Christ was Jesus.' (Acts 18:27f.) His approach to things evidently appealed to some more than that of Paul who must have appeared simplistic by comparison. He personally had no intention of dividing the church, and he certainly had no quarrel with Paul.

We do not know if Peter actually paid the church a visit – Paul often called him by his Aramaic name 'Cephas' – or if some had come from Palestine claiming to be true to his particular position which, they said, was different from that of Paul or Apollos. (Paul would have denied that. He claims to be in complete accord with Peter as far as the basic gospel message was concerned. 'Whether then it was I or they, so we preach and so you believed.' 1 Corinthians 15:11.) Certainly some were using Peter's name as their party cry, while it could be that others, no doubt with an eye to originality, claimed to be nothing but Christ's!

In the early chapters of 1 Corinthians (1–3) Paul points out the emptiness of high sounding intellectualism while at the same time complaining that their divisions were merely a sign of their spiritual immaturity. They may have been born again but they had remained at baby stage. In practice there was nothing to choose between them and unconverted people. 'While there is jealousy and strife among you, are you not of the flesh, and behaving like ordinary men?' (1 Corinthians 3:3.) What they had not grasped was that each minister had a different job to do as far as the church was concerned. Some may plant the seed, others may follow up by watering it, but only God can make it grow (1 Corinthians 3:6f.). All were at the service of the church, hence Paul could write (1 Corinthians 3:21–23):

> All things are yours, whether Paul or Apollos or Cephas or the world or life or death or the present or the future, all are yours; and you are Christ's; and Christ is God's.

The church belongs to no man; it is the property of Christ.

Heresy

The most serious divisions within the churches were over theological issues, that is, differences in teaching and sometimes plain heresy. The word 'heresy' originally meant a particular opinion, after which it came to mean a sect or a party (e.g. 'the party of the Sadducees' Acts 5:17; 'the party of the Pharisees' Acts 15:5). However, it also had a doubtful ring about it, and we find Christians being described by the term when the Jews wanted to accuse them. Paul is called 'a pestilent fellow, an agitator ... and a ringleader of the sect of the Nazarenes' (Acts 24:5). Even so this did not necessarily close the discussion. The Jews at Rome were prepared to listen to Paul's opinions even though they said that 'with regard to this sect we know that everywhere it is spoken against' (Acts 28:22).

When the word is used from the context of the Christian faith it is always in its sinister sense. It was quite legitimate to have different opinions on a variety of issues, but when the central truths of the faith were involved it was no longer opinion; it was heresy. It is spoken of as 'a work of the flesh', in Paul's terms, a product of sinful, fallen human nature ('party spirit' Galatians 5:20). It is seen as 'destructive' (2 Peter 2:1), and Christians are told to avoid it as 'unprofitable and futile' (Titus 3:9).

We certainly see the baleful effects of heresy and erroneous teaching in the New Testament. The church at Colossae had been exposed to teaching which belittled the Lord Jesus Christ and laid all kinds of needless rules on the Christians there. The Philippians were also perplexed by a group who might have been perfectionists, that is, claiming that they had 'arrived' spiritually, or libertines, kicking over the traces and living immorally (Philippians 3:12–21). Some Thessalonians had been led astray concerning the timing of the second coming of the Lord Jesus Christ. When Paul begs them 'not to be quickly shaken in mind or excited, either by spirit or by word, or by letter purporting to be from us,' (2 Thessalonians 2:2) he implies that the false teachers were either claiming special revelation or even working a deliberate fraud. The letter to the Hebrews is the story of the temptation which some Jewish Christians were feeling, to give up the Christian faith and to lapse back into the old ways. One practical effect was that of making them stay away from Christian meetings (Hebrews 10:25). In 2 Peter and Jude we read of a subtle heresy which combined Christian profession and immoral living, which evidently had great appeal.

John had to warn his friends of 'antichrists' who would lead them astray, and who had evidently seceded from the church. 'They went out from us, but they were not of us; for if they had been of us, they would have continued with us; but they went out, that it might be plain that they all are not of us.' (1 John 2:19.) In this sense, of course, division might be described as inevitable and necessary. Paul uses a similar argument: 'there must be factions among you in order that those who are genuine among you may be recognised' (1 Corinthians 11:19). In fact, on some occasions we might even speak about the responsibility to part company with some who contradict the faith. John counselled his friends that if anyone came to them teaching error they were not to 'receive him into the house or give him any greeting; for he who greets him shares his wicked work' (2 John 10f.). Unfortunately over the years, as in New Testament times, Christians have used this principle to divide over secondary issues and thus unchurch one another when they ought to have been one in Christ.

We have this illustrated for us in what must have been one of the most serious issues which threatened to divide the church at large in apostolic times, and that was the demand by some that Gentile Christians had to conform to the whole Jewish law, including circumcision, if they were going to be saved. We find this reflected in several letters, (e.g. Galatians, Romans, Philippians) and in the book of Acts (15:1–35). It caused Paul on one occasion publicly to rebuke Peter and others (Galatians 2:11–14) and it was only settled by a gathering of the apostles and the Jerusalem church elders (Acts 15). At that meeting there was 'much debate' which was settled by the straight testimony of experience. Peter related the strange way in which God had taught him that no man was 'common or unclean' during his visit to the Gentile Cornelius (Acts 10). The Gentiles were good enough for the Lord even if they were not good enough for the Jews. God had mercy on both without distinction, and the Holy Spirit endorsed that fact. Paul went on to tell of his own work with Barnabas, and of what God had done among the Gentiles. Regardless of the views of some, God was bless-ing and saving non-Jews. James summed up the discussion by reminding them of the scripture promises about God's future work among the Gentiles, and by proposing a working compromise. Gentiles were to be welcomed, but they must show evidence of real repentance from their old ways, and they must be sensitive to the scruples of their Jewish brethren.

It is probably as the aftermath of this controversy, or at least of the practical problems arising from mixing Jews and Gentiles in the same churches, that Paul spent considerable time in his letters writing about scruples, that is, personal rules of conduct. (See 1 Corinthians 8–9; Romans 14:1 – 15:13.) He was aware that because of their vastly different upbringings, Jewish and Gentile Christians had widely differing attitudes to a whole variety of things, like the food they were free to eat, or the days they observed as special. Paul's general argument is that the gospel brings liberty from legalistic requirements like these, and that it is 'the weaker brother' who still feels committed to such regulations. However, in love we must not only welcome one another because Christ has welcomed us irrespective of our background, we must be considerate to the point of waiving our freedom and rights lest we unnecessarily offend 'a brother for whom Christ died'.

He also has some sharp words for those who were pleading their freedom as an excuse for getting involved in the pagan world from which they had been saved. Such involvement could easily compromise the gospel and commit them to activities which were diametrically opposed to their new found faith. Paul's bid for peace in such a situation involved a loving and intelligent re-appraisal by both sides. Neither need be right and both were responsible for the practical outworking of their unity in Christ. There was never any suggestion of separate Jewish and Gentile churches. That would have been defeat. These issues were secondary, and they had the potential to deal with them to the glory of Christ.

Apostolic authority

In both the theological and practical controversies which threatened to divide the New Testament churches, the apostolic confidence and authority is striking. Paul could speak about 'the authority which the Lord has given me' (2 Corinthians 13:10), and when his own gospel was questioned, he could appeal to the common ground he had with the other apostles. It was not a matter of 'believe what you will'. There was a common, agreed body of belief which the apostles claimed had been given to them from God himself, a faith 'once for all delivered to the saints' for which they had to contend (Jude 3). In the white-hot Galatian situation, Paul made it abundantly plain that the content of the gospel was not ill-defined or optional: 'Even if we, or an angel from heaven, should preach to you a gospel contrary to that which we preached to you, let him be accursed.' (Galatians 1:8.)

The apostles were sure that they had the truth. 'We are of God,' says John. 'Whoever knows God listens to us, and he who is not of God does not listen to us. By this we know the spirit of truth and the spirit of error.' (1 John 4:6.) Likewise Paul: 'If any one thinks that he is a prophet, or spiritual, he should acknowledge that what I am writing to you is a command of the Lord.' (1 Corinthians 14:37.) It is significant that 'the apostles' teaching' is mentioned in the same breath as 'fellowship' after Pentecost (Acts 2:42). It is evident from what we have been reviewing that not all Christians had a full grasp of the whole Christian revelation, but it is equally plain that there were certain cardinal points in the apostolic message which were irreducible and irreplaceable. There was a 'standard of teaching to which [they] were committed' (Romans 6:17), and deviation from it spelt heresy and division.

The traditional description of the church has been 'one holy, catholic and apostolic' and the last term has been variously explained at different times in the history of the church. It is reasonably plain that in biblical terms it is true in so far as the church is committed to the authoritative teaching of the apostles. In the New Testament such teaching and fellowship were inseparable. To deny one was to deny the other (1 John 1:3).

6

CHURCH MEMBERSHIP

Having admitted that the New Testament churches had problems, we must also recognize that they were the problems of life and not, as is so often the case with ourselves, the problems of a dead or a dying organization. We might have examples of 'cooling down' reflected in the letters to the seven churches, (Revelation 2–3) but in the early days there was something spontaneous about the fellowship which stands in sharp contrast to many of our present day nominal church memberships. For all our so-called progression and the refinements of our organization, we often lack the vitality which comes across the years to us from the pages of Scripture.

When trying to understand any group of people it is necessary to ask at some stage, 'Who were eligible for membership?' Membership itself, of course, although used in general terms nowadays, was originally part of the picture of the body. A member is a limb, so we must now enquire just who were the limbs, that is, who were the people who made up the membership of the church in those days. Once again we must try to put aside any modern preconceptions of what 'church membership' implies, and try and go back to the original scene in order to reconstruct it in our understanding.

Disciples

In terms of Jesus' life and ministry, those who formed the

circle of his followers were those who had been confronted by his claims and who had responded to the challenge. Early on in the gospel records we have the account of Jesus' command of 'Follow me!' to the fishermen by the lakeshore (Matthew 4:18–22) and to the tax collector in his office (Matthew 9:9). We read that such was his appeal that they 'immediately' left all to follow him, although Luke tells us that, in Peter's case, this was accompanied by a deep sense of unworthiness after the miraculous catch of fish (Luke 5:1–11). Jesus' call involved the promise of service: 'Do not be afraid; henceforth you will be catching men.'

It is clear that Jesus made quite sure that those who identified themselves with him understood the terms on which they came. To one eager would-be disciple he cautioned, 'Foxes have holes, and birds of the air have nests; but the Son of man has nowhere to lay his head.' (Luke 9:58.) Calling another to follow him and being met with the excuse that the man concerned must delay his response until he had fulfilled the filial duty of caring for and burying his father, Jesus' words seemed hard: 'Leave the dead to bury their own dead; but as for you, go and proclaim the kingdom of God.' (Luke 9:60.) To the man who would follow him but first begged leave to say goodbye to those at home Jesus said: 'No one who puts his hand to the plough and looks back is fit for the kingdom of God.' (Luke 9:62.)

On another occasion when Jesus' symbolic teaching about his death caused offence, instead of softening the situation, he continued to sift the chaff from the wheat by making the issue of discipleship a hard one. Many could not take it. 'This is a hard saying,' they said. 'Who can listen to it?' ... 'After this many of his disciples drew back and no longer went about with him.' (John 6:60, 66.) So by his initial call and then by his continued demands and teaching, Jesus appears to have turned away many in the great crowds who flocked to him but who could not accept the terms of his discipleship. These included whole-hearted allegiance to himself which cut across any other claim or tie, however legitimate that responsibility might seem. Discipleship answers to lordship, nothing less, and in this we have often erred in our modern preaching. We have offered salvation on easy terms. At times, Jesus could not have made it much more difficult. He wanted people who meant business and who would last when things got difficult. He wanted personally committed disciples.

Converts

It is at this point that there is direct continuity between the teaching of Jesus and that of his followers. They also called for wholehearted commitment to Christ. This was 'conversion', or literally 'turning'. Paul says that Christ sent him to the Gentiles 'to open their eyes, that they may turn from darkness to light and from the power of Satan to God, that they may receive forgiveness of sins and a place among those who are sanctified by faith in me' (Acts 26:18). He summed it up elsewhere as 'repentance to God and ... faith in our Lord Jesus Christ' (Acts 20:21). Repentance was a change of heart leading to an open break with past sins. He makes it quite clear that it is more than sorrow for sin. They had to 'perform deeds worthy of their repentance' (Acts 26:20), a similar demand to that of the 'preacher of repentance', John the Baptist. ('Bear fruits that befit repentance,' Luke 3:8.) This meant that if their sorrow was real it would be expressed in a change of behaviour. As far as converts from paganism were concerned this would mean a radical 'about-turn', but for Jews also it was part of a recognition of their failure to see God's purpose in Christ when he came.

Believers

Faith in the New Testament is a comprehensive term. It includes the acknowledgement of certain facts about Christ. John concentrates on the truth that 'Jesus Christ has come in the flesh' (1 John 4:2), while Paul lists among the 'terms of the gospel' the facts of Christ's death for sins, his burial and his resurrection on the third day (1 Corinthians 15:1–5). Again more was required of pagans with their background of 'many "gods" and many "lords"' than of Jews who, at least, believed in the one Creator God (1 Corinthians 8:5–6). We find the apostles starting 'further back' with them, preaching God from creation and providence and then moving on to Christ and his gospel (e.g. at Lystra in Acts 14:15–17 and at Athens in Acts 17:22–31).

From James' outburst about faith, it looks as though some had been content to let the matter rest there (James 2:14–26). He complained of some whose 'faith' was no more than an intellectual assent to the facts, what we would call belief *about* God. With a rather cutting remark he comments, 'You believe that God is one; you do well. Even the demons believe – and shudder.' (James 2:19.) So it is fairly plain that mere professed belief was not regarded as enough for salvation and, consequently, for church membership. (The New Testament writers would not have distinguished between the two. There was no salvation outside the church in the sense in which we have defined it.)

Some have felt that James' insistence on works as well as faith contradicts Paul's affirmation that salvation is by faith and not works. On studying the subject a little closer, however, it is apparent that they are using the terms in different ways. As we have seen 'faith' for James is 'mere belief'. When he called for works he was saying that real faith carries over into action, and if there is no action, no change in behaviour, the person is simply deceiving himself. The 'works', then, are necessary evidence of the genuineness of the 'faith'. 'Show me your faith apart from your works,' he challenges them, 'and I by my works will show you my faith.' (James 2:18.)

When Paul says, 'By grace you have been saved through faith; and this is not your own doing, it is the gift of God – not because of works, lest any man should boast,' (Ephesians 2:8f.), he is maintaining that we cannot do anything to save ourselves, that our 'works' cannot merit or earn salvation. When he uses the word 'faith' it means much more than mere belief; it practically means 'obedience'. He describes his ministry as bringing about 'the obedience of faith' among all the nations (Romans 1:5). He speaks about Christians glorifying God by their 'obedience in acknowledging the gospel of Christ' (2 Corinthians 9:13). It was the acknowledgement that Jesus Christ was their Lord and Master, and it issued in open confession: 'If you confess with your lips that Jesus is Lord and believe in your heart that God raised him from the dead, you will be saved.' (Romans 10:9.) Many have linked this open stand with baptism which, as we shall see, in New Testament times had the double significance of starting the Christian life and identification with God's people. Baptism was 'into Christ' (Romans 6:3) which, as we have noted, in Paul's language is almost saying 'into the body'.

We have all these elements coming together in a passage in Paul's letter to the Galatians (3:26–29):

> In Christ Jesus you are all sons of God, through faith. For as many of you as were baptized into Christ have put on Christ. There is neither Jew nor Greek, there is neither slave nor free, there is neither male nor female; for you are all one in Christ Jesus. And if you are Christ's, then you are Abraham's offspring, heirs according to promise.

Through faith we receive our adoption and become members of God's family. This is another way of describing baptism and 'putting on Christ' which is more than an individual affair. It introduces us to a universal fellowship which cuts across all natural barriers and gives us a real unity as we are all identified with the Lord Jesus Christ. But it is precisely here that all Christians, whether of Jewish or Gentile background, find themselves to be in true succession to the faithful saints of the Old Testament and, as such, receiving all God's promised blessings. It is when we read this kind of description that we may assume that, as far as they were able to ascertain, all the members of the church in those days would have been converted people, not merely professing Christ, but actively committed to him.

There are some who for various reasons would extend this definition to include the children of believers. This whole subject is closely connected with that of infant baptism with which we shall deal in a later section. Quite apart from the debatable issue of whether or not children were baptized, we do have injunctions in the New Testament letters addressed specifically to children. For example, children are told to obey and honour their parents 'in the Lord' (Ephesians 6:1–3) or because it pleases the Lord (Colossians 3:20). (This is a decidedly 'double-edged' argument, since if they were old enough to respond in this way they would be old enough to believe.) In describing the children of a 'mixed' marriage, that is between a believer and an un-believer, Paul speaks of them as 'holy' (1 Corinthians 7:14). However, he also speaks of the unbelieving partner in the same way: 'the unbelieving husband is consecrated (literally: 'made holy') through his wife, and the unbelieving wife is consecrated through her husband.' It might be better to understand the whole verse as referring to the immense privileges that any unbeliever has, be they partner or child, if they live in the same home as someone who is the temple of the Holy Spirit. It is very doubtful if the apostle could have conceived of anybody being 'in Christ' without personal faith.

It appears from the book of Acts that from Pentecost, men and women were 'added' to the Christian fellowship as soon as they believed and were baptized, on the same day in fact (Acts 2:41). There was no waiting and no pre-baptismal or pre-membership classes. This was logical if to be 'in Christ' was to be 'in the body'. Conversion, coming into Christ, would then equal church membership. It follows that, ideally, there were no Christians who were not baptized and church members; there were no church members who were not converted and baptized.

But what if the evangelists or the converts were mistaken

in their confession? It is possible in such circumstances for people to make a profession of faith which is not genuine and, moreover, has had no time to prove itself as true. It does seem that mistakes could be made in this respect and we may even have an example of this in the book of Acts. At Samaria along with the many who responded to Philip's evangelism, Simon the magician also believed and was baptized (Acts 8:9–13). However, when Peter and John came from Jerusalem, they made it fairly obvious that he had no legitimate place within the church and no rightful claim to the benefits of the gospel. 'You have neither part nor lot in this matter,' they said, 'for your heart is not right before God. Repent therefore of this wickedness of yours, and pray to the Lord that, if possible, the intent of your heart may be forgiven you.' (Acts 8:21f.). Some have argued that the words do not necessarily deny his conversion, but it might be more natural to understand them as describing 'an un-converted church member'. The request that brought the apostles' retort, that he might buy the gift of the Holy Spirit with money, seems to indicate that he had not grasped the central issues of the gospel at all.

John also laments some who 'went out from us' but were 'not of us' (1 John 2:19), evidently referring to some who had originally identified themselves with the church but who had lacked the root of the matter. Peter speaks of false teachers who go as far as 'denying the Master who bought them' (2 Peter 2:1), while Jude says that 'admission has been secretly gained by some who long ago were designated for ... condemnation' (Jude 4).

The church visible and invisible

Because of all this the concept of a converted church has been felt by many to be an impractical ideal. There must always be a mixture of those who are genuinely converted and those who are deceiving themselves and others by a false profession in the church. Scripture may provide evidence for this. Jesus' parables are bluntly realistic when they describe the response to the gospel. Only the seed that fell into good ground bore fruit, although that which fell on rocky ground, as well as that which fell among thorns, showed some signs of life (Matthew 13:3–9, 18–23). The parable of the weeds among the wheat may also speak of the mixture in the church (Matthew 13:24–30), with the command to leave well alone until the harvest time. (This is not the only interpretation of this parable. In his explanation, Jesus did describe the field as 'the world' (Matthew 13:36–43), which has led some to maintain that it is really a description of the good and evil in the world which will only be sorted out at the Judgement.) The parable of the drag-net (Matthew 13:47–50) might tell the same story. Jesus warned his disciples in the Sermon on the Mount against 'false prophets who come to you in sheep's clothing but inwardly are ravenous wolves' (Matthew 7:15). He also cautioned those who professed him as Lord and yet did not actually obey. On the judgement day they would claim to have served him in dramatic ways – 'Lord, Lord, did we not prophesy in your name, and cast out demons in your name, and do many mighty works in your name?' – to which the Lord will have to reply that he never knew them, that is, he never recognized them as his own (Matthew 7:21–23).

One might even add the example of Judas Iscariot who, though numbered among the inner circle of Jesus' disciples, was certainly not 'of them'. 'Did I not choose you, the twelve,' said Jesus (John 6:70), 'and one of you is a devil?' He could claim that he had lost none of those whom the Father had given him except 'the son of perdition, that the scripture might be fulfilled' (John 17:12). There are questions about Judas' call and fall that we shall probably never be able to answer, but at least he does illustrate the possibility of being known as a disciple while being far from God in his heart.

In the last analysis, only 'the Lord knows those who are his' (2 Timothy 2:19), although, as the verse continues, those who claim to be his, who 'name the name of the Lord', should 'depart from iniquity'. The only test we have for the genuineness of anyone's profession is the evidence of their lives. As Jesus said, 'You will know them by their fruits.' (Matthew 7:16.) When we see evidence of a true spiritual experience, we may, by rule of thumb, say that someone really belongs to the Lord, but ultimately only he knows. Peter could say of Cornelius and his friends, 'God who knows the heart bore witness to them, giving them the Holy Spirit just as he did to us;' (Acts 15:8), but we have to admit that the case is not always as clear.

This risk of having people identified with the church who are not truly the Lord's led traditionally to the distinction between the 'visible' and the 'invisible' church. The visible church is the church as we see it, a mixed company of *professing* people, but containing both true and false. The invisible church is the true church, the company of those who are the Lord's and really born again. The difference will only be revealed on the judgement day, and until that time we have to deal with the situation as it is, and not as we would like it to be.

Although the New Testament never makes the distinction in these terms, there is some truth in this. It was certainly the case with God's ancient people, the Jews. They depended heavily on their natural heritage and privileges, and both Jesus and the apostles, not to say John the Baptist, hurt and offended them by telling them that something more was required. Jesus warned them, 'There you will weep and gnash your teeth, when you see Abraham and Isaac and Jacob and all the prophets in the kingdom of God and you yourselves thrust out.' (Luke 13:28.) He had to tell Nicodemus, that representative of sincere Jewry, that he had to be born again if he was going to enter the kingdom of God, a privilege which Nicodemus had no doubt taken for granted previously (John 3:1–15).

In his attempts to show the Scripture basis for his gospel, Paul maintained that to be a true Jew was not something outward, but something inward (Romans 2:25–29). 'Not all who are descended from Israel belong to Israel,' he said (Romans 9:6). This would have been as startling to many of the Jews of the day as the present-day assertion that being born into a Christian home and reared in a Christian way does not necessarily make one a Christian. In Paul's way of thinking it could even be a drawback. He had to list all the privileges in which he had once confided, and then write them off as liabilities in that they held him back from commitment to Christ (Philippians 3:4–8). No inherited privilege can ever substitute for personal faith. If Paul had to say to his own generation, 'Examine yourselves, to see whether you are holding to your faith,' (literally: 'to see if you are in the faith' 2 Corinthians 13:5), how much more would he have to challenge those of us who have assumed our Christianity as part of our cultural heritage?

The early years

The real possibility of error in the faith-baptism-membership pattern may well have led to the development of what we call the catechumenate early on in the history of the church. These were groups of people under instruction, preparing for baptism and church membership. The aim was to make sure that they understood the basics of belief – something increasingly important as the church moved out into the pagan Gentile world – and that they grasped the terms of their commitment. Some scholars have argued that this pattern was already being followed in New Testament times. Some of the material, they say, fits well into a suggested programme for a pre-baptismal class, and the very word seems reflected at one point. ('Let him who is taught [*katechoumenos*] ... share ...with him who teaches [*katechounti*],' Galatians 6:6.) Perhaps, like us, the apostles were prepared to deal with the real rather than the ideal situation, probably even learning the hard way and making provisions for the problems that arose. They certainly must have spelt out the claims of Christ clearly, as they could appeal to such a baptismal commitment in their later teaching (e.g. Romans 6:1–4).

Did they have membership lists, or did they just assume that once they belonged to the church they might identify themselves with any local church? Most certainly the latter, as we find Paul, for example, greeting Christian friends he had known in other circumstances in a church which he had never yet visited (Romans 16:3–15). The natural assumption is that when they travelled, they simply linked up with the group of Christians where they went. We know that, in this connexion, some took letters of recommendation from the church to which they were currently attached, or which had sent them (2 Corinthians 3:1). Whether or not there were actual membership lists is open to question. They certainly knew who belonged to them and who did not. Paul could write about 'outsiders', that is, those who were still in the world and not in the church (1 Corinthians 5:12). John speaks about those who had left the church as having gone out (1 John 2:19), so it is clear that, list or no list, the boundaries between the church and the world were fairly well drawn.

Membership, however, was not only a matter of initial commitment. They had to go on as they had begun, and we do not have to read far in the New Testament letters to realize that some did not. Although it was the apostles' ambition to 'present every man mature in Christ' (Colossians 1:28), there were always those who did not progress as rapidly as they ought. This was Paul's concern with the Corinthian church members. Before conversion they had been incapable of receiving spiritual truth, 'unspiritual' or 'natural' men and women (1 Corinthians 2:14). After conversion they ought to have grown from spiritual babyhood into mature believers (1 Corinthians 2:6, 15), or 'spiritual' people, guided and controlled in their behaviour by the Holy Spirit. As it was they had marked time and were still 'men of the flesh' or 'carnal'. The tell-tale symptoms were that in their behaviour

they were just like the unconverted, 'like ordinary men'
(1 Corinthians 3:1–4). Perhaps after the problem of the
unconverted church member, the carnal church member
comes next. There was no question about their conversion.
They knew the gospel and had experienced the power of
the Holy Spirit, and yet they had not progressed. Paul charges
them, warns them and breaks his heart over them, just as
he would react, no doubt, to many of our present day churches
suffering from the same malaise. Even to be genuinely converted and in the church is no ground for complacency. We
must be moving on. The Hebrew Christians were similarly
described as those who had not grown up, as spiritual 'Peter
Pans'. 'By this time,' they were told (Hebrews 5:12), 'you
ought to be teachers,' but 'you need some one to teach you
again the first principles of God's word. You need milk, not
solid food. . . .' And so the author appeals to them, 'Let us
leave the elementary doctrines of Christ and go on to
maturity' (Hebrews 6:1).

For those who gave heed there was every hope of improve-
ment and growth. There were some, however, who saw no
inconsistency in professing Christ and being identified with
his church and yet living like the unconverted. What of those
whose behaviour was an embarrassment to other Christians?
When the straight appeal of teaching and rebuke failed, the
apostles had to rely on sterner measures, on what has come
traditionally to be called 'church discipline'.

7

BAPTISM

When the risen Christ commanded his disciples, 'Go ... make disciples of all nations, baptizing them...' he was only extending what they had already been doing during his ministry. John tells us that one of Jesus' strategic moves from the hostile south to the more friendly north was because he knew 'that the Pharisees had heard that Jesus was making and baptizing more disciples than John'. He goes on to add that 'Jesus himself did not baptize, but only his disciples' (John 4:1f.), although presumably it must have been on his behalf and with his approval. This links the rite with Jesus' forerunner, John the Baptist, who as all the gospels tell us, called on the crowds to express their repentance in this way as a prelude to the ministry of One who was to come after him.

The baptism of John

Great numbers had gone out from the towns and villages to be baptized by John 'in the river Jordan, confessing their sins' (Matthew 3:6). 'I baptize you with water for repentance,' he said, 'but he who is coming after me is mightier than I, whose sandals I am not worthy to carry; he will baptize you with the Holy Spirit and with fire.' (Matthew 3:11.) The record goes on to tell us of Jesus himself coming to John to be baptized, of John's hesitation which implied that Jesus had no sins to repent of, and of Jesus going down into the water along with the sinners of his own generation (Matthew

3:13–16). It was a most important event in Christ's career as it was accompanied by the descent of the Spirit and marked the beginning of his public ministry.

For our purposes, however, it is more important to ask where John got the idea of baptizing from. He does not explain the rite and yet the Jews seemed to know what he was about. There must have been some preparation for it although our evidence is not as complete as we would like it to be at present. We do know, of course, that ceremonial washing was part of Jewish ritual. We have instructions about a variety of washings in the Old Testament, and we know that they formed part of Jewish custom at the time of Christ. Jews often chose a site near a river or the sea for their places of prayer for that reason, although ceremonial washing came short of actual baptism.

Although our evidence is somewhat later than the New Testament, we also know that when a man was converted from paganism to Judaism, the ritual involved circumcision, baptism and sacrifice. He was immersed along with his family as a token that the filth of his pagan past was washed away. Many have suggested that this practice was adopted in the time of Christ and, if it was, it would account for the Jewish leaders' angry reaction to John the Baptist. He would have been requiring of born Jews what was otherwise reserved for pagans. As we have seen, his very words seem to question their confidence in their natural descent: 'Do not presume to say to yourselves, "We have Abraham as our father"; for I tell you, God is able from these stones to raise up children to Abraham.' (Matthew 3:9.)

We also know that the monastic community down by the Dead Sea at Qumran was baptizing people at about the same time. Some have suggested that John the Baptist might have had strong links with this group in his childhood, and others have maintained that they hold the key to Jesus' teaching as well. However, these ideas are far from proven. If anything, the evidence runs the other way, as their laws and way of life were vastly different from the gospel that Jesus preached, or even John's message. The importance of their writings is that they throw a flood of light upon the way in which first century Jews were thinking, and on the subject in hand they remind us that baptism was no new thing for the Jews of Jesus' time. They already had some idea of what it meant.

Christian baptism

Baptism was not only an aspect of Jesus' earthly ministry; he quite clearly commanded that it should be part of the future apostles' continuing mission after he had left them. They were told to 'make disciples of all nations, baptizing them in the name of the Father and of the Son and of the Holy Spirit,' teaching them to carry out all that they had been told (Matthew 28:19f.). When we read about their fulfilment of that commission from Pentecost onwards, baptism is mentioned fairly frequently.

After Peter's preaching on the day of Pentecost 'those who received his word were baptized' (Acts 2:41). When Philip preached to the Samaritans many believed and 'were baptized, both men and women'; and as we have already seen, even the notorious Simon was baptized (Acts 8:12f.). While the same Philip was explaining the gospel to the Ethiopian official in his chariot, the man exclaimed, 'See, here is water! What is to prevent my being baptized?' and commanding the chariot to stop, Philip baptized him there and then. (Acts 8:36, 38.) Ananias' words to the shattered Paul in Damascus were: 'And now why do you wait? Rise and be baptized, and wash away your sins, calling on his name,' (Acts 22:16), and we are told that he was baptized even before 'he took food and was strengthened' (Acts 9:19).

Peter, forced against his inbred prejudice to preach the gospel to the Gentile Cornelius, is astonished when the Holy Spirit falls upon the group, but concludes: 'Can any one forbid water for baptizing these people who have received the Holy Spirit just as we have?' (Acts 10:47.) On Paul's second missionary journey at Philippi, a businesswoman called Lydia intently listens to his preaching. 'The Lord opened her heart to give heed to what was said by Paul. And ... she was baptized, with her household.' (Acts 16:14f.) In the same town, the jailer, wakened about midnight by the earthquake, and terrified lest his charges had escaped from the half demolished jail, heard the gospel and at 'the same hour of the night ... was baptized at once, with all his family' (Acts 16:33). Further along the road, at Corinth, 'Crispus, the ruler of the synagogue, believed in the Lord, together with all his household; and many of the Corinthians hearing Paul believed and were baptized' (Acts 18:8), while at Ephesus Paul finds a group of people who had already been baptized 'into John's baptism'. They had evidently heard of the preaching of John the Baptist and had responded. Paul goes on to tell them the whole story, about Christ, and then baptizes them again (Acts 19:1–5).

We may conclude that, for the apostles, baptism was no optional extra for which some applied and about which others did not bother. Jesus had commanded it and they required it of those who responded. Peter's Pentecost appeal was 'Repent, and be baptized every one of you in the name of Jesus Christ for the forgiveness of your sins...' (Acts 2:38). He 'commanded' Cornelius and his friends 'to be baptized in the name of Jesus Christ' (Acts 10:48). When Paul wrote even to churches he did not found, he could assume that all professing Christians had been baptized and could base his argument on that fact. He questions the Christians in Rome about the implications of their baptism: 'Do you not know that all of us who have been baptized into Christ Jesus were baptized into his death?' (Romans 6:3); and to the Colossians he can say, 'You were buried with him in baptism...' (Colossians 2:12).

The distinctive feature about Christian baptism was that it was 'in the name of the Father and of the Son and of the Holy Spirit' (Matthew 28:19), or 'in the name of Jesus'

(Acts 2:38, 10:48, 19:5). There seems to be no studied difference between the fuller and the shorter phrases. In practice they seem to imply the same thing, that is, truly Christian baptism in contrast to any other baptism. The phrase 'in the name of' was used legally in those days in a similar way to today. We speak about a piece of property being 'in someone's name' when we mean that they are the legal owners. To be baptized into someone's name equally meant to be baptized into their ownership or into allegiance to them. This is illustrated for us by one of Paul's arguments with his 'problem children' at Corinth. You will remember that they had divided the church under the labels of the different preachers who had come to them: 'Each one of you says, "I belong to Paul," or "I belong to Cephas,"' and so on. Paul questions their understanding of the basic gospel. 'Is Christ divided?' he asks. 'Was Paul crucified for you? Or were you baptized in the name of Paul? I am thankful that I baptized none of you except Crispus and Gaius; lest anyone should say that you were baptized in my name.' He then adds as an afterthought that he did also baptize the household of a certain Stephanas, although he cannot remember if that was all he baptized. 'For,' he says, 'Christ did not send me to baptize but to preach the gospel....' (1 Corinthians 1:12–17.)

By this last remark he is not belittling baptism as some have suggested, nor must we imply that he only baptized some of his converts. The fairer reading of the situation, when we compare the passage with other references to baptism, is that he baptized a few, and then delegated the job to someone else. This practice paid dividends in the case of the Corinthians, because Paul could legitimately say that he was not collecting personal disciples. They did not belong to him, they belonged to Christ and had demonstrated that fact by being baptized in Christ's name. As they all owed their allegiance to no one but Christ, they ought to have realized just how petty their human divisions were. Only Christ had died for them, and they were his alone, a fact that we also need to remember today when a minister is tempted to build a church round the attraction of his own personality.

The meaning of baptism

The most natural symbolism of baptism appears to be that of cleansing understood in spiritual terms as forgiveness. 'Be baptized ... for the forgiveness of your sins,' Peter told the Pentecost crowd (Acts 2:38). 'Rise and be baptized, and wash away your sins,' Ananias advised Paul (Acts 22:16). This would take on even greater significance for those who came to Christ from a pagan background. Before conversion the Corinthian Christians had shared the vices of their own day. 'But,' says Paul, 'you were washed, you were sanctified, you were justified in the name of the Lord Jesus Christ and in the Spirit of our God.' (1 Corinthians 6:11.) The implication of verses like these is that baptism formed part of the original preaching of the gospel. The Ethiopian's question as to whether he could be baptized indicates that, along with Philip's explanation about Christ and his death, he must have said that a proper response to the gospel involved baptism (Acts 8:35–37). When the writer to the Hebrews appeals to them to 'leave the elementary doctrines of Christ and go on to maturity,' he includes in the list a reference to 'instruction about ablutions' or literally 'baptisms' (Hebrews 6:1f.). The reference here may be to Jewish washings, or it may be to a comparison between Christian baptism and any other kind of ceremonial bathing. It seems to have formed part of the basic A-B-C of gospel teaching.

As we have seen, perhaps the most striking aspect of the New Testament practice was that converts were baptized straight away without waiting, and apparently without much instruction. This in turn gives us a clue to what baptism meant in those times. It was part of the conversion response to the gospel. Peter speaks of it in this way. He has been using the illustration of Noah which suggests the idea of being 'saved through water', and he continues; 'Baptism, which corresponds to this, now saves you, not as a removal of dirt from the body but as an appeal to God for a clear conscience [or possibly 'an answer to God from a clear conscience'] through the resurrection of Jesus Christ.' (1 Peter 3:21.) If we understand New Testament baptism as a prayer acted out for forgiveness, or an enacted response to the claims of Christ, we shall not be far from the truth. Ananias' advice to Paul to be baptized, washing away his sins and 'calling on his name' (Acts 22:16), contains the same idea. As we know, the New Testament response to the gospel was a commitment of faith. Baptism expressed that commitment. This is why Peter did not say at Pentecost, 'Repent and believe,' but rather, 'Repent and be baptized,' (Acts 2:38). We know that many of our earliest creeds go back to baptismal services where the candidate for baptism was required to confess his faith. As church history became more and more theologically complicated, these creeds became more comprehensive, but originally they were probably very simple. It has been suggested that Paul's statement, 'if you confess with your lips that Jesus is Lord and believe in your heart that God raised him from the dead, you will be saved,' (Romans 10:9) probably reflects a baptismal confession.

Baptism and conversion

Baptism and conversion are closely related in the New Testament. Paul may have them both in mind when he refers to 'the washing of regeneration and renewal in the Holy Spirit' (Titus 3:5), and some have seen a similar meaning in Jesus' statement, 'unless one is born of water and the Spirit, he cannot enter the kingdom of God,' (John 3:5, although this is not the only interpretation of the verse). If we use the technical expression 'baptismal regeneration', we must be very careful to qualify it, or we shall find ourselves reading later church theology into it. Baptism certainly did not automatically confer salvation. As Peter says it is 'not as a removal of dirt from the body' (1 Peter 3:21), not like an external bath, and Paul has to remind the Corinthians that baptism in itself is no guarantee of their salvation. Speaking of the Old Testament people of God he says that 'all were baptized into Moses in the cloud and in the sea' just as they experienced many other privileges in their desert wanderings. 'Nevertheless with most of them God was not pleased; for they were overthrown in the wilderness.' (1 Corinthians 10:1–5.) Paul presses the lesson home by saying that 'these things are warnings for us, not to desire evil as they did' (1 Corinthians 10:6), and the most natural implication is that baptism is useless unless accompanied by that change in behaviour which we have described as genuine conversion.

Because of this link between baptism and the radical change which marks the beginning of a Christian life, Paul could use the symbolism of baptism in an extended way (Romans 6:3f.):

> Do you not know that all of us who have been baptized into Christ Jesus were baptized into his death? We were buried therefore with him by baptism into death, so that as Christ was raised from the dead by the glory of the Father, we too might walk in newness of life.

He similarly writes to the Colossians about being 'buried with him in baptism, in which you were also raised with him through faith in the working of God, who raised him from the dead' (Colossians 2:12). Most agree that the idea of dying, being buried and rising again was suggested by going beneath the water and emerging from it. Some would even argue that the taking off and putting on of clothes for the ceremony suggested theology for Paul. ('You have put off the old nature with its practices,' Colossians 3:9; 'Put on then, as God's chosen ones...' Colossians 3:12.)

For the apostle baptism spoke of our close identification with Christ. It was 'baptism into Christ', a phrase which relates closely with Paul's whole understanding of the Christian life as being 'in Christ'. By faith and the indwelling Holy Spirit we are so at one with Christ that what he did may be credited to us. In fact, we may be described as dying and rising *with* Christ. Paul's argument then continues as an appeal to 'die' and 'rise' with Christ in practice, denying the dictates of our fallen human natures and yielding ourselves to Christ in ready obedience (Romans 6:1–14). Baptism becomes a model for the ongoing life of the Christian.

However, as we have seen, Christian experience always has a corporate as well as an individual aspect. For Paul to be 'in Christ' is almost the same as saying 'in the body', that is, in the church. Because of this baptism is not just a personal response or a personal confession of faith. It was a rite of initiation into the church: 'you ... were baptized into Christ, ... you are all one in Christ' (Galatians 3:27f.). Once again, this was not an automatic or mechanical affair. It had to be effected by the Spirit. 'By one Spirit we were all baptized into one body – Jews or Greeks, slaves or free – and all were made to drink of one Spirit.' (1 Corinthians 12:13.)

It is in this respect that the old definition 'an outward and visible sign of an inward and spiritual grace' probably holds good for the New Testament practice of baptism. Could you have the sign without the grace? Yes, unfortunately, if Simon the Magician was not really converted (Acts 8:13, 21). You could certainly pass through a form of baptism without being a Christian, as the Ephesian disciples of John the Baptist discovered when Paul not only preached the full gospel to them, but also baptized them again (Acts 19:1–5). Because their first baptism did not fulfil all the requirements, it was simply not Christian baptism. Could you have the grace without the sign? Once again, yes, for Cornelius and his friends were manifestly converted before baptism, even though Peter saw to it that the situation was made good straight away (Acts 10:44–48).

Infant baptism

There seems to be no distinct or explicit evidence for

baptizing children in the New Testament – in fact we have
no clear reference to it until the second century – but some
scholars have argued that the silence does not necessarily
mean that it was not practised. The children, at least the
boys, of parents involved in the Old Covenant received circumcision which was the sign of the covenant. It might follow
that, by analogy, the children of Christian believers were
baptized for their parents' faith. For those espousing this
'covenant theology', the Old and the New Covenants are
really only two phases of the same covenant, that of grace.
On this basis, baptism is simply circumcision updated. Paul
describes Abraham's circumcision as 'a sign or seal of the
righteousness he had *by faith* while he was still uncircumcised' (Romans 4:11). Abraham was adult when he was
circumcised, but his family – and their successors – were
not. However, if it is a case of 'baptism equals circumcision',
we might expect to find more about it in the New Testament,
especially where there are long debates about the necessity
or otherwise of circumcision. In fact, baptism and circumcision are only related in one reference: 'In him [Christ] also
you were circumcised with a circumcision made without
hands, by putting off the body of flesh in the circumcision
of Christ; and you were buried with him in baptism,'
(Colossians 2:11f.), a notoriously difficult passage to understand, which, whatever else it might mean, does not say that
baptism is Christian circumcision.

In this connexion, a great deal is sometimes made of the
way in which Jesus received and blessed little children when
he was here in the flesh. 'Let the children come to me,' he
said, 'do not hinder them; for to such belongs the kingdom
of God.' (Mark 10:14.) If Christ welcomed little children in
this way, it is argued, surely he still does; to which some
would reply that he did and he does, but that he did not
baptize them.

One of the strongest arguments for infant baptism is based
on the references in the book of Acts to household baptism,
where it seems as though the whole family was baptized when

the parents believed. On closer inspection the case is still far from clear. All Cornelius' household had received the Spirit (Acts 10:47). All the members of the Philippian jailer's family had heard the gospel (Acts 16:32). In the case of Crispus at Corinth, all the family had believed (Acts 18:8), while the household of Stephanas, whom Paul remembered he had baptized at Corinth, are also described as converts (1 Corinthians 1:16, 16:15). The only ambiguous case is that of Lydia at Philippi (Acts 16:15), and she appears to have been a businesswoman who might have been unmarried. Additional evidence, as we have seen, might be material in the letters addressed to children as belonging to the Lord, so that their baptism may be assumed. (As we have noted, the reference to children of a mixed marriage as being 'holy' (1 Corinthians 7:14) is no more evidence for their baptism and church membership than that of the unbelieving partner.)

In favour of 'family baptism', we may say that the family was a much more closely knit unit in those days than it is in the western world today. The husband and father would act on behalf of the whole as he does in some parts of the world still. Faith would be a family affair, and whole families would come over to the gospel. There was a family solidarity which we have lost, and this might stand behind the New Testament references. On the other hand, we know all too well that the gospel could equally divide the family unit. Jesus warned that he had come to bring division rather than peace. 'Henceforth in one house there will be five divided, three against two and two against three; they will be divided, father against son and son against father, mother against daughter and daughter against her mother, mother-in-law against her daughter-in-law and daughter-in-law against her mother-in-law.' (Luke 12:51–53.) It was a happy experience when the whole family came to Christ, but sadly it did not, and it does not, always happen that way. Equally, although a parent's faith was a great privilege for a son or daughter, it was no guarantee that the rising generation would believe for themselves.

Early practice

We only have hints in the New Testament of the actual method of baptizing someone in those days. If John's baptism is anything to go by, we know that it took a great deal of water. An incidental reference tells us that while Jesus and his disciples were baptizing in Judea, 'John also was baptizing at Aenon near Salim, because there was much water there;' (John 3:22–23). It seems easiest to picture Jesus' baptism by John in terms of immersion. After being baptized 'he went up immediately from the water,' (Matthew 3:16). Similarly with the Ethiopian official: 'They both went down into the water, Philip and the eunuch, and he baptized him. And when they came up out of the water...' (Acts 8:38f.).

Paul's teaching about dying and rising with Christ seems to be based on the same method, while the word itself comes from a root meaning 'to dip', which was also used in the dyeing industry for the immersion of cloth in vats of dye.

It has been argued that the phrase 'to baptize with' might be understood at times in the looser sense of 'pouring upon' or 'deluging'. This might be the key to its metaphorical use. 'Are you able to drink the cup that I drink,' Jesus asked James and John, 'or to be baptized with the baptism with which I am baptized?' (Mark 10:38; Luke 12:50.) The cup signified the lot or purpose which God had appointed for him; the baptism the overwhelming experience of his death. This might point to the practice of standing the person being baptized in the water and pouring water over him. One can envisage situations where denied the ideal amount of water, they used what they had as a symbol. In fact we do have evidence for this happening in the second century, although the same source makes it quite plain that total immersion was the preferred method.

Baptism for the dead

While dealing with baptism, we must take into account a

curious reference which is part of Paul's argument for resurrection. Having established the fact of Christ's resurrection
and said that ours follows, he then adds: 'Otherwise, what
do people mean by being baptized on behalf of [or 'for']
the dead? If the dead are not raised at all, why are people
baptized on their behalf [or 'for them']?' (1 Corinthians
15:29.) There is no parallel teaching about this 'baptism for
the dead' anywhere else, and we have to fall back on a whole
variety of suggestions as to what might have been its meaning.
Did it mean baptism on behalf of someone who had died
unbaptized (which is how the Mormons understand it)? Was
it baptism because of the testimony of someone who had died
as a believer? Or was it something else? The answer must
be that, at present, we simply do not know. It must have
been plain to the Corinthians, or Paul would not have used
it as part of his argument, but we do not as yet have the
background which they had, and even with all the suggestions
we must confess our ignorance.

8

QUALITY CONTROL

Excommunication

The Reformers saw what they called 'church discipline' as one of the marks of the true, that is the biblical, church. How correct were they? Just what did happen to Christians who did not live up to an acceptable Christian standard in New Testament times? The simple answer would be that, given due warning and admonition, the unrepentant member was put out of church fellowship.

This was not a novel solution. Christians could find precedent in the Old Testament. Ezra had to take the community which returned from exile to task for inter-marriage with their pagan neighbours. In a spirit of deep penitence, the people resolved to put matters right, and Ezra put out a proclamation calling all the returned exiles to an assembly at Jerusalem to rectify the matter. The condition was that, if anyone did not respond, 'by order of the officials and the elders all his property should be forfeited, and he himself banned from the congregation of the exiles' (Ezra 10:1–8).

This became standard practice at a local level among the synagogues of Jesus' time. One source tells us that initially the reprobate was excluded for thirty days, which gave him the opportunity to repent and get things right. If he did not respond in that period, it was extended by two further months, following which the offender faced a complete ban both from the synagogue and from Israel. The monastic community by the Dead Sea at Qumran was even stricter.

A member could be excluded for a period there if he laughed noisily or if he fell asleep during a session!

'Blessed are you,' said Jesus, 'when men hate you, and when they exclude you' (Luke 6:22) meaning, from the synagogue. We have on record the account of at least one who was turned out because of his allegiance to Jesus. The parents of the man born blind, whom Jesus healed, refused to answer for him because 'the Jews had already agreed that if anyone should confess him to be Christ, he was to be put out of the synagogue' (John 9:22). The man himself met that fate when he honestly and simply testified to what Christ had done for him. 'They answered him, "You were born in utter sin, and would you teach us?" And they cast him out.' (John 9:34.)

This kind of sanction against the misbehaving member was already in operation when Jesus spoke about it for his own followers, and later when the apostles saw to it that it was exercised among the churches. One of the two 'church' references in Jesus' teaching was in this context. He spoke of the occasion when two disciples have a difference (Matthew 18:15–17). If possible, it should be made up between them and go no further: 'If your brother sins against you, go and tell him his fault, between you and him alone. If he listens to you, you have gained your brother.' (Verse 15.) But what if he will not listen? Then you need help in the form of 'one or two others' who will go with you 'that every word may be confirmed by the evidence of two or three witnesses' (verse 16). However, if this does not achieve the desired reconciliation, the church should be told. If the offender will not listen to the local assembly, there is no further possibility. The unyielding member should be regarded 'as a Gentile and a tax collector' (verse 17), that is, as an outcast as far as the community is concerned.

Paul counsels similar treatment for some at Thessalonica who were refusing to pull their weight and earn their living. Paul himself gives them due warning about the inconsistency in their behaviour (2 Thessalonians 3:12): 'Such persons we command and exhort in the Lord Jesus Christ to do their work in quietness and to earn their own living.' If this failed to do the trick, that is, if they refused to obey what the letter said, Paul tells the others to 'note that man [probably referring to some public decision] and have nothing to do with him' (2 Thessalonians 3:14). They were to 'keep away' from such (2 Thessalonians 3:6). However, this was not to be seen as a hopeless situation but rather a means of bringing him to repentance. It was done 'that he may be ashamed' and get his priorities sorted out. In spite of his false values they were not to regard him as an enemy, 'but warn him as a brother'. (2 Thessalonians 3:14–15.)

We find the same action recommended to Titus when some were unrepentantly divisive. 'After admonishing him once or twice, have nothing more to do with him,' says Paul (Titus 3:10). 'Such a person is perverted and sinful; he is self-condemned,' (Titus 3:11), that is, his behaviour was so out of place in a Christian fellowship that in reality he judged himself. Timothy is advised that if some 'persist in sin', he is to 'rebuke them in the presence of all, so that the rest may stand in fear' (1 Timothy 5:20). Discipline sometimes has a healthy effect on others in the fellowship who may have been tempted to do the same things.

In more drastic cases, Paul speaks of a more drastic remedy. He describes this as delivering the culprit to Satan (1 Corinthians 5:5; 1 Timothy 1:20). We have the whole process laid out for us in the first Corinthian letter (chapter 5). There it was a serious case of incest, a matter which would have shocked even the permissive pagans of the day. The church should have taken action without Paul's prompting, but because they had not, he tells them that they must put the matter in hand straight away (1 Corinthians 5:4f.):

When you are assembled, and my spirit is present, with the power of our Lord Jesus, you are to deliver this man to Satan for the destruction of the flesh, that his spirit may be saved in the day of the Lord Jesus.

It was to be the action of the assembled church, not just the church officers. They had both Paul's approval and Christ's authority in doing this, but the difficulty lies in the actual formula which he uses. 'Delivering to Satan' is not the easiest terminology to understand, and it has called out a variety of comments. Some suggest that it meant some kind of miraculous curse, but probably a better way of understanding it is in terms of putting the person out of church membership. Paul had said, 'Let him who has done this be removed from among you,' (verse 2), and he concludes the chapter with 'Drive out the wicked person from among you' (verse 13). Inside the church they were under Christ's jurisdiction. They had been 'delivered ... from the dominion of darkness and transferred ... to the kingdom of his beloved Son,' (Colossians 1:13), from Satan's realm to Christ's. The discipline involved being put back into the world, back under Satan's sway.

The purpose of this extreme action is also described in difficult terms. Paul tells us that it is for 'the destruction of the flesh' (1 Corinthians 5:5). 'Flesh' is a term which we may take more than one way in Paul's writings. It could refer to a man's body and therefore to his physical health. We certainly have hints of physical penalties in those days. The immoral Jezebel at Thyatira would be 'thrown on to a sick bed' together with her companions as a result of her perversions, for although she had been given time to repent, she had refused (Revelation 2:20–22). The terrible judgement of Ananias and Sapphira was physical (Acts 5:1–11), while Paul pointed out to the Corinthians themselves that their ungodly behaviour at the Lord's Supper had already resulted in sickness and even death (1 Corinthians 11:30). Whereas the Bible dissuades us from making, in general terms, a direct connexion between a person's sin and their suffering, there does seem to be some ground for understanding Paul's words here in this way.

But Paul also often uses the term 'flesh' in the sense of fallen, sinful human nature, and that could also be understood in this passage. The exclusion from fellowship might be designed to bring the man to terms with his sinfulness and lead him to repentance. Paul tells us that he took the same action with Hymenaeus and Alexander 'that they may learn not to blaspheme' (1 Timothy 1:20). Certainly the purpose of the Corinthian discipline was intended to be remedial. It was so that 'his spirit may be saved in the day of the Lord Jesus' (1 Corinthians 5:5). Even in such a case of open wickedness there was still hope of repentance, and it seems from Paul's second letter to the church that the action was effective (2 Corinthians 2:1–11). He appears to be talking about the same man when he speaks about someone who has caused both him and the church pain. It was an anguished time but 'for such a one this punishment by the majority is enough' (verse 6). They should now rather 'turn to forgive and comfort him' or he might be completely 'overwhelmed by excessive sorrow' (verse 8). Indeed, they need to take this action or Satan might gain the advantage over them, no doubt meaning that a hard and unforgiving attitude in such a case could equally be used by the devil.

Discernment

The whole subject raises the question as to a Christian's qualifications for judging other members of the church. Jesus quite clearly censured a judging spirit (Matthew 7:3f.):

> Why do you see the speck that is in your brother's eye, but do not notice the log that is in your own eye? Or how can you say to your brother, 'Let me take the speck out of your eye,' when there is the log in your own eye?

Paul himself told the same Corinthians not to 'pronounce judgement before the time, before the Lord comes' (1 Corinthians 4:5). As the Lord alone can read the hidden motives that lie behind behaviour, he alone is qualified to judge. On these grounds, many would hesitate before they passed judgement on a fellow Christian. They are too conscious of their own sinfulness and limitations.

But then, Jesus also told his disciples to be discerning. In the same sermon, he tells them not to give dogs what is holy or throw their pearls before swine (Matthew 7:6), not the most flattering descriptions of people. Paul goes on from the passage on discipline to point out that Christians were perfectly well qualified to sort out differences between church members. They should not 'dare to go to law before the unrighteous instead of the saints' (1 Corinthians 6:1). The saints would judge the world – and angels – and they should be prepared to exercise that discretion here and now. Perhaps the safeguard in cases of church discipline was the fact that it was corporate and not just individual action. The church together dealt with outrageous behaviour or blatant inconsistencies within its membership, and it did it for its own sake. Paul was evidently concerned for the witness of the church among its pagan neighbours. If the Corinthians tolerated not only sub-Christian but sub-pagan standards, what did they have to offer? It killed their witness stone dead. Peter tells his friends that, although it was no disgrace to suffer for being a Christian, no professing Christian should 'suffer as a murderer, or a thief, or a wrongdoer, or a mischief-maker' (1 Peter 4:15).

The other reason for strong action at Corinth was that such tolerated sinfulness had a corrupting influence on the whole church. 'Do you not know,' asks Paul, 'that a little leaven leavens the whole lump? Cleanse out the old leaven...' (1 Corinthians 5:6f.). It was not just the witness of the church but the whole quality of church life that was at risk. Just as we have a positive mutual ministry when it comes to building one another up, we may also influence one another in harmful ways. Tolerated sin is just like yeast permeating the whole batch of dough. That should be enough to make us want to take action.

This does not mean, of course, that there should be a regular 'witch-hunt' among church members. Jesus' words

might apply here, as we have seen, when the servants were
eager to gather the weeds from the wheat field. There was
always a danger of rooting up the wheat along with them
(Matthew 13:28f.). Our discernment is sometimes so restrict-
ed that we find it easy to unchurch the saints along with
the sinners.

In general, although church discipline was exercised in the
New Testament churches, it appears to have been the rare
occurrence rather than the regular practice. It was the
ultimate sanction after all other efforts to put the matter
right had failed. Even then, it was done in the hope that the
offender might be awakened to the gravity of his position
and return in repentance. While Christians are commissioned
to take this kind of action, their own attitude had to be that
of forgiven sinners. They were to deal with others as Christ
had dealt with them (Ephesians 4:32), aware that even
correcting another involved temptations to personal pride and
a censorious spirit. Paul tells the Galatians that 'if a man
is overtaken in any trespass' the 'spiritual', or those in good
standing, 'should restore him in a spirit of gentleness [or
'meekness']'. They should look to themselves or they also
will be tempted (Galatians 6:1). It is all too possible quickly to
condemn one's own sins in another.

While on the subject of judgement, we must not forget
that Christ, as head of the church, exercises his own judgement and discipline. In the book of Revelation, it is the risen
Christ who takes the churches to task, along with individuals,
and calls them to repentance (Revelation 2–3). If they do
not put things right, his ultimate sanction is to 'remove the
candlestick', or to write off that particular fellowship
altogether. Christians do not, any more than the Old Testament saints, have any ground for sitting back and assuming
that all is well. Paul warns the Gentile Christians with his
picture of the olive tree, that just as the natural branches
were broken off that they, the wild branches, might be grafted
in, the reverse is also possible. 'If God did not spare the
natural branches, neither will he spare you.' (Romans 11:21.)

Peter also speaks about judgement beginning 'with the household of God' (1 Peter 4:17), although in his letter this seems to refer to the period of persecution which they were about to endure. In their case, as in the case of all proper discipline, the end result would not be loss but gain. It was that their faith 'more precious than gold which though perishable is tested by fire' might 'redound to praise and glory and honour at the revelation of Jesus Christ' (1 Peter 1:7). Churches, as well as individual Christians, need to learn not to despise 'the discipline of the Lord' (Hebrews 12:5).

9

GOD'S EXCLUSIVE POSSESSION

The holy church

Our discussion of church discipline has filled out, in practical terms, the traditional description of God's people as 'one, holy, catholic and apostolic', because we have really been talking about the holiness of the church. This widely used biblical word means, at heart, 'separation'. It is used in Scripture of anything that is 'separated' from the ordinary use of the world for God's exclusive use. That is why it can be used of both things and people. In the Old Testament places were holy, buildings were holy, even the pots and pans in the Temple were described as holy.

When it came to people, it involved considerably more, because people are not like things. They have wills of their own, and so if any person was to be holy, he must have surrendered his will to God. This is God's great concern: to call and create a people who would be wholly his in heart and mind and body, his exclusive possession. This is what redemption is all about, Old Testament and New Testament. God redeemed his people from Egypt, that is, he bought them out of slavery in order to make them his own. God redeems his people from the dominion of Satan and sin for the same reason, 'that we should be holy and blameless before him' (Ephesians 1:4), that we should be wholly his.

From the New Testament point of view, the ransom price has been paid. 'In him we have redemption through his blood,' says Paul (Ephesians 1:7). 'You know that you were ransomed ... not with perishable things such as silver or gold, but with the precious blood of Christ,' says Peter (1 Peter 1:18f.). Because of this, God is calling into existence a people who will be truly his, a holy people, and this is the ideal description of the church.

The purity of the church as God's exclusive possession is well illustrated by various titles given to God's people, many of which carry over from the Old Testament. Paul's great assertion was not that he had abandoned his Old Testament heritage, but that he had found its fulfilment in Christ. Christians were the true spiritual successors of people like Abraham, 'Abraham's offspring, heirs according to promise' (Galatians 3:29). They were the true Jews. 'We are the true circumcision,' he claims, 'who worship God in spirit, and glory in Christ Jesus, and put no confidence in the flesh' (Philippians 3:3). Circumcision, the sign of the covenant, is not an external thing at all. 'He is not a real Jew who is one outwardly.... He is a Jew who is one inwardly, and real circumcision is a matter of the heart, spiritual and not literal.' (Romans 2:28f.) 'Neither circumcision counts for anything, nor uncircumcision, but a new creation,' and so he can wish 'peace and mercy ... upon all who walk by this rule, upon the Israel of God' (Galatians 6:15f.).

Because of this, one of the regular titles for Christians in the New Testament letters is that of 'saint'. 'Saint', like 'sanctify' or 'consecrate', comes from the root meaning 'holy'. A saint is someone who has been set apart for God's possession and use, which as we have seen is the ideal for God's people. They were called saints whether they lived it out in practice or not. Paul writes to that headache of a church at Corinth and addresses the letter 'to those sanctified in Christ Jesus, called to be saints' (1 Corinthians 1:2). As we shall see, the very title laid responsibilities upon them to work it out in real life. It was a name to live up to.

Peter strings together several Old Testament titles when describing the church. 'You are a chosen race, a royal priesthood, a holy nation, God's own people [literally 'a people

for his possession']' (1 Peter 2:9). It had not been their idea
or choice. It had been God's. He had set his love upon them
and chosen them, just as he had loved and chosen that rabble
of slaves in Egypt when he brought them out to make them
a nation and give them a land of their own. In a similar way,
'Once you were no people but now you are God's people;
once you had not received mercy but now you have received
mercy,' (1 Peter 2:10). This means that Hosea's prophecy
of restoration for God's people had found its fulfilment in
the church (Hosea 1:6f.; 2:23). They were 'a royal priesthood'
because through Christ they had access to God and were
set apart for his worship, as Peter says, 'that you may declare
the wonderful deeds of him who called you out of darkness
into his marvellous light' (1 Peter 1:9). Above all they must
be a holy nation, a people who were especially God's own,
which is the meaning of the old fashioned phrase 'a peculiar
people', not 'odd' but 'God's'.

These titles, this call and choice, are frequently the ground
for the apostles' appeal to actual holy living. 'As he who
called you is holy, be holy yourselves in all your conduct,'
writes Peter; 'since it is written, "You shall be holy, for I
am holy."' (1 Peter 1:15f.) Paul reminds the Corinthians
(2 Corinthians 6:16–18) that God said,

> I will live in them and move among them, and I will be their God,
> and they shall be my people. Therefore come out from them and
> be separate from them, says the Lord, and touch nothing unclean;
> then I will welcome you, and I will be a father to you, and you
> shall be my sons and daughters . . .

Having such promises, he concludes, we must 'cleanse ourselves from every defilement of body and spirit, and make
holiness perfect in the fear of God' (2 Corinthians 7:1). The
apostle makes it quite clear elsewhere that this is not a call
to monastic living. We have to associate with sinful people
in the ordinary rough and tumble of life or 'we would need
to go out of the world' (1 Corinthians 5:10). By the grace
of God we have the potential to live up to our high calling

within the framework of a fallen world. They had to be in the world and yet not of it, or as Peter puts it, 'aliens and exiles' (1 Peter 2:11).

This idea of not belonging here, of being pilgrims on the way to the promised land, comes out well in an epistle like that written to the Hebrews. Reviewing the heroes of faith, the author says in effect that God's people are always 'strangers and exiles on the earth.... They desire a better country, that is, a heavenly one. Therefore God is not ashamed to be called their God, for he has prepared for them a city.' (Hebrews 11:13–16.) The ideas of homeland and holy city, of course, come straight from the Old Testament, and are found elsewhere in the New Testament description of God's people. Paul speaks about 'the Jerusalem above' (Galatians 4:26), while John sees a vision of 'the holy city, new Jerusalem' (Revelation 21:2) in all its splendour prepared for the perfected saints at the end.

Because Philippi was a Roman colony in northern Greece, Paul could translate the idea into Gentile terms when he wrote to them. The church is also a colony, he says, a colony of heaven. 'Our commonwealth [or 'citizenship'] is in heaven,' (Philippians 3:20). Because the church is an outpost of heaven, Paul can also appeal to them to live 'worthy of the gospel' (Philippians 1:27), and so fulfil their duties as citizens of heaven.

As we have seen, a good number of Old Testament pictures are used to illustrate the New Covenant blessings. As Israel had been God's vine, Christ was the vine and they were the branches (John 15:1–11). As Israel had been the Lord's flock, Christ was the shepherd, a regular Old Testament description of a ruler, and they were the sheep (John 10:1–18). Another frequently used image is that of the Temple.

The Temple of God

For the Jews, the Temple at Jerusalem had been the centre

of national faith and worship, and as a building, in Jesus'
day, the source of considerable pride. Jesus, however, foretold
that the days of a particular place for worship were coming
to an end. When the Samaritan woman tried to introduce
a 'theological' question into her discussion with Jesus as to
where God wanted them to worship, Jesus cut her short
(John 4:21–23):

> Woman, believe me, the hour is coming when neither on this
> mountain [for the Samaritans had worshipped on Mount Gerizim]
> nor in Jerusalem will you worship the Father.... True worshippers
> will worship the Father in spirit and in truth.

He explained that God, being spirit, was not confined to any
one place. True worship was spiritual, and required not
Temple and ritual, but worshippers 'in spirit and in truth'.
Stephen got into trouble for taking a similar line in his defence
before the Council (Acts 7:48–50), and God was finally going
to endorse the words of his Son and his servant by the
terrible judgement of A.D. 70, when the Temple was razed
to the ground by the Romans crushing the Jewish revolt.

In the epistles, the whole emphasis has shifted from a place
to a people. Because of the indwelling Holy Spirit, the very
bodies of individual believers could be described as his
temples (1 Corinthians 6:19), a fact which was a powerful
moral incentive when it came to the use or abuse of their
bodies. But the term is also used collectively. With rather
mixed metaphors, Paul paints a picture for the Ephesians
of a building, not made with materials, but of individuals
(Ephesians 2:19–22):

> You are ... built upon the foundation of the apostles and prophets,
> Christ Jesus himself being the cornerstone, in whom the whole
> structure is joined together and grows into a holy temple in the
> Lord; in whom you also are built into it for a dwelling place of
> God in the Spirit.

The building is made up of believers. Christ is described
as the cornerstone as that was the stone which bound the

walls together. Once again, he is the cohesive, unifying factor in the church. The apostles and prophets are involved in their foundational ministries, and the whole structure is still growing as numbers increase.

Peter uses the same idea when he speaks of Christ as the living stone, rejected by men but chosen by God, and of Christians as living stones too, 'built into a spiritual house, to be a holy priesthood, to offer spiritual sacrifices acceptable to God through Jesus Christ' (1 Peter 2:4f.). This meant in practice that they were not only the true successors to the Old Testament priesthood, but that buildings as places of worship were entirely secondary. Where two or three met together in Christ's name, he was among them and they together were the spiritual Temple of God.

The picture is used slightly differently by Paul when describing the work of different ministers in one church, once again at Corinth (1 Corinthians 3:10–17). With Christ as the foundation, for there can be no other starting-point for genuine church growth and life, each minister is seen as a builder erecting a structure upon it. Some build cheaply. Their work does not cost them much. It is wood, hay and stubble. Others take care and build with expensive and durable materials, gold, silver and precious stones. The final judgement is likened to fire which sweeps the building, burning up the results of unworthy service while leaving the lasting work. Paul then rams the message home. Did they not know that they were God's Temple and that God's Spirit dwelt in them? Destructive behaviour in the church, then, is like sacrilege. Those who violate God's Temple invite God's wrath.

The bride of Christ

The idea of the exclusive relationship of marriage as applied to God's people is likewise found first of all in the Old Testament. The prophets' complaint was that Israel had sinned although God had been a husband to them (Jeremiah 31:32), and their rebellion is often described in terms of spiritual adultery. Paul draws on the same theme when he describes the church as the bride of Christ. He became concerned for the faithfulness of Christians because, he says, 'I betrothed you to Christ to present you as a pure bride to her one husband' (2 Corinthians 11:2). They should belong to Christ alone.

He develops the idea in an extended passage where he is giving advice to Christian married couples (Ephesians 5:21–33). As the husband loves the wife, so Christ loves the church, to the point of giving himself for her. As the wife is subject to her husband, so the church should be subject to Christ, owning his lordship and following his lead. Christ is concerned, as any husband might be, with the purity of his bride. Because of this his ongoing work in the church is one of progressive sanctification, making the church in practice the holy entity it ought to be. There is a reference to 'the washing of water' which may refer to baptism, although it is further qualified by 'with the word' (verse 26). Christ's aim is 'that he might present the church to himself in splendour, without spot or wrinkle or any such thing, that she might be holy and without blemish' (verse 27).

At this point Paul combines the idea with that of the church as the body of Christ. Man and wife become one flesh. 'No man ever hates his own flesh, but nourishes and cherishes it, as Christ does the church,' (Ephesians 5:29). It is difficult to see at times if Paul is more concerned with marriage as an illustration of the church, or the reverse. The central idea is obvious, however, for as marriage shuts a man or woman off from any other sexual relationship, the church is ideally separated to Christ and Christ alone.

The holy city

In the book of Revelation the image of the bride is also combined with another, but this time it is that of the holy city (Revelation 21). Here we have a double picture of spiritual purity realized and of God dwelling among his people. 'Behold, the dwelling of God is with men. He will dwell with them, and they shall be his people, and God himself will be with them,' (verse 3). The Last Judgement is over, and only those written in the Lamb's book of life comprise his bride and dwell in his city. God's Old Covenant people are represented in the construction, and so are the apostles. It is a picture of life and light in the presence of God, the church as she ought to be and as one day she will be. In the meantime the work must continue, and when John comes back to earth it is the bride issuing the invitation to sinners to come to Christ and to drink of the water of life (Revelation 22:17).

The call of grace

It would have been readily admitted by those who first used them that these descriptions of the church's holiness are ideal, and that they will only come to fulfilment at the end when Christ completes his work in the church. They are, however, an indication of the high privileges which God's people enjoy even here and now, privileges which they should live up to. The theme of the New Testament exhortations is often 'Become what you are!' 'You are God's people, therefore live holy lives separate from the evil world around you!' 'You are God's Temple, set apart for his exclusive use and demanding a reverence and care when serving or behaving within the fellowship.' 'You are Christ's bride, and therefore you must be pure and worthy of your bridegroom.' Underlying all these images is the sense of God's purpose and God's call. Sanctification was not a matter of self-improvement, any more than Christians were their own making. It was all of grace, as only God could call and only God could work his work within the lives of the individual men and women who made up the whole. However, this laid certain responsibilities upon those called to live in a manner worthy of their vocation.

10

THE CHURCH
AND ORGANIZATION

Through the years there have always been those who have
maintained that any organization within the church is a matter
of spiritual decline from the original practice and pattern.
The New Testament church, it is held, was directly dependent upon the guiding of the Holy Spirit, and therefore had
no need of organizational structure. Others have felt that even
within the New Testament itself, we have a decline from the
original, free and unstructured ideal (such as we might find
reflected in the Corinthian correspondence) to the rather more
realistic organization with church officers and all that goes with
them (as we find in Paul's letters to Timothy and to Titus).
Neither view does justice to the New Testament.

Jesus' group of disciples itself, although small and flexible,
was not entirely unorganized. Within the twelve there was an
'inner circle' of three, Peter, James and John, who were
particularly close to Jesus, and who accompanied him on
special occasions like the transfiguration (Mark 9:2) and in the
garden of Gethsemane (Mark 14:33). We know that they lived
from a common fund because Judas Iscariot is mentioned as
treasurer (John 12:6; 13:29). We know that there were certain
women attached to his party who 'ministered to him' (Mark
15:40f.), while the errands of the Twelve and the Seventy
required a certain amount of organization (Matthew 10;
Luke 10:1–20).

The first Christians were all Jews and had the pattern of
the synagogue as part of their regular life and worship. As

we have seen, the word 'synagogue' is actually used once for the church gathering (James 2:2). Although church and synagogue structures were different, the latter, in God's providence, did a great deal to prepare God's people for group worship detached from the Temple. As far as we can see, first-century synagogue organization was simple and functional, the sort of organization we find reflected in the churches of that time.

Reading the New Testament letters and the book of Acts, we see the beginnings of church organization. They met together. They taught the new converts. They celebrated the Lord's supper. They also lived out of a common fund, in Jerusalem at least. At Ephesus there appears to have been an order, or at least an authorized list, of widows dependent on church support. They sorted out their own grievances. They set apart and commissioned their missionaries. They supported their workers and their wives. They made collections for poorer churches and sent the gifts with specially appointed church delegates. They chose and appointed their own officers, on one occasion when the practical difficulties of the hour revealed the need. We read of apostles travelling between the churches, of elders and of deacons. The churches themselves exchanged letters. They also called a representative council to settle issues of church-wide importance ... there is enough to show us that there was certainly some organization.

One of the problems facing us in assessing this evidence is that the organization has no clearly discernible pattern. For example, it is very difficult to see how churches related to one another, and to what degree they were autonomous units, acting on their own. It is not easy to see what role the Jerusalem church played in regulating the affairs of other churches. They most certainly held a council there on the issue of Gentile converts, when they made certain recommendations to the churches and disowned some who had been teaching differently. (Acts 15:24 – 'We heard that some persons from us have troubled you with words, unsettling your minds, although we gave them no instructions. . . .') On the other hand,

the apostle Paul argues strongly for his independence from the
Jerusalem church and seems to care little for their opinion
(Galatians 1:6–2:10).

It is equally difficult to find out just what authority or
ministry was exercised within the local groups by the different
church officers named. Whereas we may conclude certain
general principles about the order of the New Testament
churches, the actual organizational pattern, and how each one
fitted into it, is not entirely clear. Perhaps this in itself might
be an indication that what organization existed was light and
functional. Certainly the structure was secondary to the life
expressed through it. The new wine had new wine-skins.

It is because of this ambiguity that most denominational
developments over the years have claimed the support of the
New Testament for their particular pattern of church life, often
emphasizing certain aspects of the biblical picture at the expense
of others. Conversely, other groups have maintained that we
have insufficient evidence in the New Testament, and that we
may therefore look to the patterns of church government which
evolved after the apostolic age for our guidance. Some go
further, and argue that the church was commissioned to
develop its own organization as time and circumstance
demanded. In this book we must concern ourselves with what
the Bible says about the organization of the early church,
although sometimes developments immediately after the New
Testament period may shed light on areas of doubt.

However little we know about the day-to-day running of
the churches in those days, we do get frequent glimpses of
the people involved, and as the church is (in our definition)
made of people, perhaps this is all for the best. Before we
turn to the specific 'offices' within the church, it would be
good to remind ourselves also that there was no clergy/laity
distinction in those days. Whereas some had special jobs to
do, including leadership, *all* (it was assumed) had received some
gift, or could do so, and therefore *each* member had some
ministry to offer.

The force of the Joel prophecy quoted by Peter on the day

of Pentecost was that, whereas under the Old Covenant only the exceptions like kings, judges and prophets had been gifted by the Spirit, a new day had dawned when all God's people would be blessed and equipped in some way or other, sons and daughters, young and old, menservants and maidservants (Acts 2:16–18). This gifting of the Spirit which we have come to call his 'charismatic' ministry (from the Greek word *charisma* meaning 'gift of grace') became evident in the ongoing life of the churches. It was easy to abuse even in those days, and it is the charismatic disorder at Corinth which gives us a great deal of insight into the use of these gifts (1 Corinthians 12–14).

Undue emphasis appears to have been placed on the gift of tongues, that linguistic extension of a person's faculties for praise or prayer, and Paul's whole point is that there are a wide variety of gifts which should all have a complementary place in the life and worship of the church. As we have seen, it is here that he introduces the picture of the body with its mutually dependent limbs. Just as we need all the members in our bodies, so all have a place within the church. No man or woman has a monopoly of the gifts. 'Are all apostles?' he asks. 'Are all prophets? Are all teachers? Do all work miracles? Do all possess gifts of healing? Do all speak with tongues? Do all interpret?' (1 Corinthians 12:29f.), and the answer he would expect every time is 'No'.

Therefore everyone is necessary for the full life of the whole, and the man with fewest gifts is as important as the man with most, while no one has them all. What is more, Paul continues to point out that they find their meaning only in a *loving* fellowship, where Christians know that they belong together, and where they minister to one another. We may speak with all the tongues imaginable, prophesy, boast of our spiritual insight, exercise miracle-working faith, give away all that we have even to the point of self-sacrifice, but without love we are nothing and we achieve nothing, even though we do it in a noisy way! These gifts were tools to use and not toys to play with. Their concern, above everything else, should have been the spiritual 'upbuilding' of the fellowship, and not merely self-expression. 'Let all things be done for edification,' says Paul (1 Corinthians 14:26).

It has long been held by many Christians that most of these gifts were withdrawn from the church after the apostolic age, on the principle that, with the completion of the canon of the New Testament, they were no longer needed. Whereas it is beyond doubt that some ministry was foundational, that God did bless the apostles in remarkable ways, and that by and large, many of the gifts did disappear from the life of the church, there is nothing in the New Testament itself which requires that conclusion. As far as Paul was concerned, in spite of the abuse of these gifts (which even led to a despising of the gifts in some places, 1 Thessalonians 5:20), a normal church would inevitably be a charismatic community with everyone involved in mutual ministry. Even when listing out special gifts of ministry, he tells us that their purpose was (literally) 'for equipping (or repairing) the saints with a view to their getting on with the work of ministry' (Ephesians 4:12).

While pointing out that everyone had something to offer, it must not be assumed that the church became a free-for-all. When it did, Paul cracked down hard. Spiritual life and its expression should be spontaneous, but that did not mean the chaotic freedom of the Corinthian situation. On the contrary, the apostle saw that it was possible to combine Spirit-led worship and ministry with a discipline which made it all the more effective (1 Corinthians 14). 'All things should be done decently and in order' (verse 40).

This meant that there was a place for specific leadership, that is, there were some who were particularly gifted to give a lead and, if necessary, to exercise discernment and restraint. Individual members were not only told to 'be subject to one another' (Ephesians 5:21), they were also told to follow the lead which their leaders gave. The Thessalonians were told 'to respect those who labour among you and are over you in the Lord and admonish you, and to esteem them very highly in love because of their work.' (1 Thessalonians 5:12f.) The

Hebrew Christians needed a similar reminder (Hebrews 13:7, 17):

> Remember your leaders, those who spoke to you the word of God.... Obey your leaders and submit to them; for they are keeping watch over your souls, as men who will have to give account. Let them do this joyfully, and not sadly....

There were, of course, particular temptations in office bearing, and we have at least one example of a man who seems to have taken over a church and was running things his way. This was a certain Diotrephes, who, John said, liked to put himself first. He would not acknowledge the apostle's authority, but rather slandered him. He refused to welcome 'the brethren' and also stopped others who wanted to do so, putting them out of the church (3 John 9f.). For some, a bad experience of leadership like this would be enough to make them argue for no leadership at all, just as a 'bad' experience of charismatic ministry might make some write it off altogether. The apostles, however, accepted both the ministry of all and the gifted leadership of individuals, controlling the first and spelling out the personal requirements of those who wielded authority in the fellowship.

11

THE APOSTLES

When Paul was listing out various ministries in the churches, he began the catalogue on two occasions with that of 'apostle' (Ephesians 4:11; 1 Corinthians 12:28). It is also evident that, when he claimed to be an apostle, he was claiming something out of the ordinary for himself, and yet we discover that this word is somewhat ambiguous when we come to define it.

'Apostle' means more than just 'missionary', although both come from the same root meaning 'to send'. The word implies rather 'someone sent on a special errand and given authority to fulfil it'. Jesus is described by the writer to the Hebrews as 'the apostle and high priest of our confession' (Hebrews 3:1) in that he came from the Father with a special commission.

The Jews had a similar word for someone sent on official business and authorized to act and speak on behalf of the sender, as a sort of proxy. Such was his delegated authority that what he did and said bound the one who sent him. The man's delegate was regarded as the man himself. With Jewish communities scattered far and wide, this kind of commission was also necessary to link them with the central Council or Sanhedrin. Although the word is not used, Paul appears to have been fulfilling exactly this function when he went to Damascus on his errand of persecution (Acts 9). He tells us that he had 'the authority and commission of the chief priests' (Acts 26:12). If this is so, then the irony of the passage is that the Lord Jesus Christ turned that apostleship into his own. Paul seems to date his calling to the task from that time.

The word was used in the general sense of a commission

when a church sent representatives to another church. The group collecting funds for the poor Jerusalem Christians were described as 'messengers [apostles] of the churches' (2 Corinthians 8:23), and Epaphroditus, the man who brought the gift from the Philippians to Paul is described in the same way (Philippians 2:25). In both cases they were sent by the fellowships with a specific job to do. However, the word is used more commonly in the special sense of 'apostle of Christ', that is, involving a particular authority deriving from him.

This authority was evidently recognized by the churches at large, and when in Paul's case it was questioned, we find him vehemently defending his qualifications. For him this special commission extended to 'the twelve' (1 Corinthians 15:5 'he appeared ... to the twelve', although there were only actually eleven at that time) and himself. 'Am I not an apostle?' he asks (1 Corinthians 9:1). 'Have I not seen Jesus our Lord?' He did recognize that his own appointment had been somewhat irregular in that he had been called to the work after the ascension of Christ. 'Last of all,' he recalls (1 Corinthians 15:8f.), 'as to one untimely born, he appeared also to me. For I am the least of the apostles, unfit to be called an apostle, because I persecuted the church of God,' a fact which seems often to trouble him.

There are times, however, when the definition seems to be broader than this. For example, it might include James, the Lord's brother, for Paul says that on his first visit to Jerusalem after his conversion, he went to visit Peter and 'saw none of the other apostles except James the Lord's brother' (Galatians 1:19). He seems to bracket Barnabas with himself when arguing for his own apostleship which would have included the right to claim financial support from the churches 'as the other apostles and the brothers of the Lord and Cephas' (1 Corinthians 9:5, although Barnabas would have been eligible for a salary on the grounds that he was a full-time worker). He links the names of Silvanus and Timothy with his own when writing to the Thessalonians, and then goes on to say that during their visit they 'might have made demands as apostles of Christ' (1 Thessalonians 1:1; 2:6, although this might only be epistolary style). Andronicus and Junias (it could even be a lady, Junia) might also qualify as they are described as people 'of note among the apostles' (Romans 16:7, although there are other interpretations of this verse), and perhaps also Apollos (1 Corinthians 4:6, 9 'us apostles'), although Paul's phraseology is just a little too loose for us to be sure.

There were certainly some who were claiming to be apostles but who were not eligible. Paul complains about 'superlative apostles' and 'false apostles, deceitful workmen, disguising themselves as apostles of Christ' (2 Corinthians 11:5, 13), and there were similar characters later in Ephesus (Revelation 2:2). He dismisses their claim and, although he attempts to establish what was genuine over against what was false, the very fact that they could make such claims might indicate that the term was used in a wider sense.

What made an apostle in the special sense? The term and the commission go back to Jesus' call of the Twelve. Luke tells us that after a night of prayer he called his disciples 'and chose from them twelve, whom he named apostles' (Luke 6:12–16). These were the Twelve to whom he gave 'authority over unclean spirits, to cast them out, and to heal every disease and every infirmity' (Matthew 10:1).

When the Eleven decided to fill Judas' vacant place, the requirements for the possible replacement were not only that he should have been with them throughout Jesus' ministry, more particularly he had to be a witness to the resurrection (Acts 1:21f.). That this idea of eye-witness evidence loomed large for them is seen in Peter's words to Cornelius: 'God raised him ... and made him manifest; not to all the people but to us who were chosen by God as witnesses...' (Acts 10:40f.). After narrowing the candidates down to two, they cast lots to decide God's mind. It was not just their human election to the office. There had to be an element of divine choice in the matter (Acts 1:23–26).

When Paul's apostleship was attacked, he majored on the risen Lord's personal commission. He had 'seen Jesus our Lord'

(1 Corinthians 9:1). The Lord had appeared to him (1 Corinthians 15:8). He went on to insist that this was direct and not mediated through any other person, group or church. 'Paul an apostle,' he writes, 'not from men nor through men, but through Jesus Christ and God the Father,' (Galatians 1:1). This had important implications for the message he was preaching. It was not a human invention or tradition: 'I did not receive it from man, nor was I taught it, but it came through a revelation of Jesus Christ.' (Galatians 1:12.) It was more than just seeing the risen Christ. Many had done that, 'more than five hundred brethren at one time' (1 Corinthians 15:6), but he does not appear to have included them in the number of the apostles.

It was the delegated authority of Christ which he claimed to exercise in the churches, the 'authority which the Lord gave' for building them up and not destroying them (2 Corinthians 10:8; 13:10). The evidence of his apostleship was 'the signs and wonders and mighty works' which he performed among them 'in all patience' (2 Corinthians 12:12) and the lasting character of his ministry. He could appeal to the Corinthians, 'If to others I am not an apostle, at least I am to you; for you are the seal of my apostleship in the Lord.' (1 Corinthians 9:2.) It is this apostolic authority which, in general terms, stands behind our collection of New Testament writings. While they were still being written, they were bracketed with Scripture (2 Peter 3:15f.).

There may be some link between this authority and 'the power of the keys' which is first mentioned when Peter confesses Christ at Caesarea Philippi. Jesus said then, 'I will give you the keys of the kingdom of heaven, and whatever you bind on earth shall be bound in heaven, and whatever you loose on earth shall be loosed in heaven.' (Matthew 16:19.) This verse has been the ground for some extravagant claims for Peter and his successors in the past. But this authority was also given to the other apostles later, where it seems to be connected with joint decisions and the authority of the group (Matthew 18:18f.). Some have paralleled it to the saying by the risen

Christ about forgiving and retaining anyone's sins (John 20:23).

The symbol of the key is an Old Testament one. Eliakim was to be steward of the king's household, and God says through the prophet, 'I will place on his shoulder the key of the house of David; he shall open, and none shall shut; and he shall shut, and none shall open.' (Isaiah 22:22.) In his case it meant the responsibility and authority of stewardship, and we may understand it similarly in the case of the disciples. They had the responsibility for preaching the gospel of Christ with its promise of forgiveness, and the authority to do so as well. It has sometimes been said that Peter exercised his power by 'opening the door of faith' to both the Jews (at Pentecost) and to the Gentiles (in the person of Cornelius), but it might be better to understand the words in the more general sense of Christ's commission. One finds a similar understanding of God-given stewardship along with authority in Paul's writings.

Most feel that the scope of an apostle's ministry was far ranging, and much wider than the local church situation. Some have argued that it would be more accurate to see their authority as limited to the churches which they themselves had planted. If that were the case, the 'false apostles' troubling the church at Corinth would have been trespassing on Paul's preserve, but it is not as clear-cut as that. Paul did have a special claim on the churches which he had founded, but we also find him working with some he did not. He did not found the church at Colossae, and yet he writes to them as an apostle (Colossians 1:1), and similarly to the church at Rome (Romans 1:5). He tells us that he did limit his ministry to certain unworked areas (Romans 15:20), and that he did so in agreement with the other apostles (Galatians 2:9), but there is no suggestion that he was limited in any other way. His concern was not to extend the sphere of his personal influence, but to preach the gospel. There is no evidence of any infallible apostolic organization or hierarchy. In fact, we have one occasion on record when Paul rebuked Peter when he was wrong (Galatians 2:11–14).

In the New Testament the apostles seem to have had a particular ministry at the very beginning of the church's history. They were part of the foundation of that spiritual Temple which replaced the old Jewish pattern, that is, the church itself (Ephesians 2:19f.). We never read about an 'apostolic succession'. The requirement of being a witness to the resurrection or that of a personal commission by the risen Christ seems to rule that out. Paul gives the impression that he was the exception that proved the rule, because he was commissioned by the Lord *after* the ascension. He calls himself one abnormally born in the apostolic family, the freak (1 Corinthians 15:8–9). Apostolic commissioning, he implied, did not normally happen that way. Again, when apostles wanted to guarantee that their message was upheld by future generations of Christians, they did not look for or appoint replacement apostles, but rather committed their teaching to those who would be faithful to it. Paul tells his delegate Timothy: 'What you have heard from me before many witnesses entrust to faithful men who will be able to teach others also.' (2 Timothy 2:2.) We may therefore conclude that New Testament apostolic succession is one of apostolic doctrine, not apostolic office.

12

VARIOUS MINISTRIES

One of our problems in working out just how the church was run in New Testament times is that sometimes ministries are described in terms of God-given abilities like 'teachers ... helpers ... administrators' (1 Corinthians 12:28), and sometimes in terms of the executive offices which the individuals held like 'bishops and deacons' (Philippians 1:1). Some dislike the idea of 'church officials' because it smacks of an institutionalism which has been so often abused in the history of the church. Their idea of the early days is an idealistic one where everybody gladly, freely and lovingly made their contribution as the Spirit led them without the need of human oversight. We certainly do have instances of the Holy Spirit leading directly. For example it was the Holy Spirit who said, 'Set apart for me Barnabas and Saul for the work to which I have called them,' at the beginning of their missionary career (Acts 13:2). After their deliberations over the Gentile Christian issue, the group at Jerusalem could write to the churches 'it seemed good to the Holy Spirit and to us...' (Acts 15:28), and on Paul's second missionary tour we have some interesting instances of the Spirit forbidding them to go in certain directions because he had other plans for them (Acts 16:6f.).

Even so, as we have seen, the idealistic view is not true to the New Testament. From the chaos which ensued at certain places, it was evident that the church needed oversight and the discipline of leadership, and this is what we find. Very early on we discover the appointment of officials alongside the apostles for certain tasks (Acts 6:3–6). At Jerusalem, the apostles evidently shared the oversight and running of the church with elders. It was the elders who received the cash gift from the church at Antioch (Acts 11:30), and we find them gathering together with the apostles to discuss the evangelization of the Gentiles (Acts 15:6). We also find Paul and Barnabas, at the conclusion of their first missionary trip, appointing elders for them 'in every church, with prayer and fasting' (Acts 14:23), indicating that from the beginning young churches were not left leaderless.

The reason for the modern reaction against church officials is that we sometimes have church leaders who appear to be devoid of spiritual ability, while those evidently gifted for the work are sometimes unrecognized, or fulfil their ministry 'unofficially'. There was no such dualism in the New Testament. There was a need for leadership in the churches, and the Lord qualified some to take that lead by gifting them in special ways. When the problem of distributing the cash arose in Jerusalem, the Apostles told the church to pick out from among their number 'seven men of good repute, full of the Spirit and of wisdom' whom they could appoint to the duty (Acts 6:3), that is, they were already spiritually qualified before they were set apart. The 'church official' without the spiritual equipment would have been a contradiction in terms in those days.

As we have seen, there were a wide variety of spiritual gifts operating in the churches then. Some stand out in this matter of leadership. After apostleship, Paul rated the gift and ministry of prophecy very highly. It was 'first apostles, second prophets' that God had appointed in the church (1 Corinthians 12:28). Like the work of an apostle, theirs was also regarded as in some way foundational – that is if the verse which tells us that the church was 'built upon the foundation of the apostles and prophets' (Ephesians 2:20) does not refer to Old Testament prophets whose words were being fulfilled as the work went on. But unlike apostleship, this gift seems to have been quite widespread, and at least a possibility for many. Having told his Corinthian friends that they should 'earnestly desire the higher gifts', Paul recommends that they pray for the gift of prophecy in particular (1 Corinthians 12:31; 14:1).

Prophets

Prophecy is probably best understood as being a direct word from the Lord to a situation or to an individual. In the Old Testament, prophets were commissioned to speak in this way with a 'Thus saith the Lord...'. We know that the New Testament ministry sometimes involved prediction. One of the Jerusalem prophets visiting Antioch, Agabus by name, 'stood up and foretold by the Spirit that there would be a great famine over all the world,' and it was this prediction which prompted the church to send their gift to Jerusalem (Acts 11:27–30). The same Agabus warned Paul on his journey to Jerusalem that the Jews would arrest him and deliver him to the Gentiles, like many of the Old Testament prophets acting out his message by binding his hands and feet with Paul's girdle (Acts 21:11). This was evidently no surprise for Paul as he had told the Ephesian elders that, although he did not know exactly what would happen there, 'the Holy Spirit testifies to me in every city that imprisonment and afflictions await me' (Acts 20:22f.).

Sometimes prophecy revealed an individual's need. Paul expected this to happen if 'an outsider or unbeliever' entered a Christian gathering: 'the secrets of his heart are disclosed; and so, falling on his face, he will worship God and declare that God is really among you.' (1 Corinthians 14:24f.) Equally it could be a word of encouragement. Judas and Silas 'who were themselves prophets, exhorted the brethren with many words and strengthened them' when they returned from the Jerusalem Council to Antioch with Paul and Barnabas (Acts 15:32). Paul describes the gift as speaking to men 'for their upbuilding and encouragement and consolation', edifying the church (1 Corinthians 14:3f.). It was evidently more than just preaching or teaching, although no doubt preaching often involves a 'prophetic' element.

In those days the gift was no respecter of persons. We find both men and women prophesying just as we do in the Old Testament. We read that Philip the evangelist 'had four unmarried daughters, who prophesied' (Acts 21:9), and Paul legislates for women who pray or prophesy in the fellowship (1 Corinthians 11:5). Sad to say, we also have false prophets mentioned. Jesus himself put his disciples on their guard against 'false prophets, who come to you in sheep's clothing' and said that, on the last day, many would claim to have prophesied in his name whom he would have to disown as not belonging to him at all (Matthew 7:15, 22f.). He said that they would be particularly active as the end drew near, and would lead many astray (Matthew 24:11). John also warns his friends that 'many false prophets have gone out into the world' and proposes that they put those to the test who claim this ministry (1 John 4:1). In that particular instance, the test was to be doctrinal. God does not contradict himself. Jesus told his disciples that they would 'know them by their fruits', evidently referring to their behaviour or to the results of their work (Matthew 7:15–20). It might have been the abuse of the gift of prophecy that caused some at Thessalonica to despise it. In some ways it is an easy ministry to counterfeit. It is difficult to answer a claim like 'This is what God says...' or 'I feel led by the Spirit...'. However, Paul counsels his friends: 'test everything; hold fast what is good, abstain from every form of evil' (1 Thessalonians 5:21f.). It is significant that another spiritual gift was 'the ability to distinguish between spirits' (1 Corinthians 12:10).

Evangelists

Whereas it was the task of the whole church to preach the good news, to evangelize, there were also some who had particular gifts in this direction. Paul lists evangelists after apostles and prophets (Ephesians 4:11), and in the book of

Acts we see one in action – Philip – who is described as 'the evangelist' (Acts 8:4–40; 21:8). We see Philip working effectively with large crowds at Samaria with many coming to faith in Christ, and equally with an individual, the Ethiopian official, bringing him to the point of commitment and baptism. Timothy also may have been among their number, for Paul tells him to 'do the work of an evangelist' (2 Timothy 4:5) and fulfil his ministry. It is interesting to note that this ability to present the gospel simply and power-fully was regarded in those days as a special gift and ministry.

Pastors

If people were brought to faith in Christ by evangelists, they grew to Christian maturity under the influence of 'pastors and teachers' (Ephesians 4:11). 'Pastoring' or 'shepherding the flock' is a well-worn biblical picture for caring for God's people. When Jesus spoke of himself as the good shepherd (John 10:11, 14), he had plenty of Old Testament precedent. He is the pastor or shepherd *par excellence*, and is called as much in the New Testament. The readers of Peter's letter had been 'straying like sheep' but had now 'returned to the Shepherd and Guardian' of their souls (1 Peter 2:25). He tells the elders to tend the flock of God willingly and worthily because one day they would see 'the chief Shepherd' who would reward them accordingly (1 Peter 5:2–5). Jesus is described in Hebrews as 'the great shepherd of the sheep' (Hebrews 13:20). Pastoring is something near to the heart of Christ himself.

Jesus commissioned the repentant Peter to do the same work after the resurrection (John 21:15–17), and set the pattern for the ministry we find illustrated in the letters and the book of Acts. The elders from the church at Ephesus were told by Paul (Acts 20:28):

Take heed to yourselves and to all the flock, in which the Holy Spirit has made you guardians, to feed the church of the Lord which he obtained with his own blood.

64009

It is a picture of guidance and nurture, of seeking the welfare of those whom God had committed to their charge. Such leadership demanded pure motives. Peter tells his pastor friends to do the job willingly and not reluctantly, with no lust for power or ambition for personal gain (1 Peter 5:2f.). The pastor was at the service of his flock, the church.

Teachers

In Paul's mind the gift of pastoring seems to be closely linked with that of teaching (Ephesians 4:11), and it would be difficult to overestimate the place of instruction in New Testament church life. In Jesus' last command, teaching his new followers to observe all that he had commanded is part of making them disciples (Matthew 28:19f.), and we find the apostles fulfilling that command from the very beginning. The converts at Pentecost 'devoted themselves to the apostles' teaching and fellowship' (Acts 2:42), being grounded in Christian understanding. We have numerous references to teaching, instruction, doctrine, truth, discernment, knowledge and so on, and the New Testament writings themselves are a striking testimony to the depth and weight of that information. If they are, as some have suggested, shortened sermons, no wonder it was possible to fall asleep through sheer exhaustion when listening to them (Acts 20:7–12)!

A Christian understanding of things was not optional. There was a 'standard of teaching' to which they were committed (Romans 6:17). Correct knowledge was seen as both a means of spiritual growth and a protection against heresy. Paul prays for his Ephesian friends (Ephesians 1:17–19) that they might have

> a spirit of wisdom and of revelation in the knowledge of him, having the eyes of your hearts enlightened, that you may know what is the hope to which he has called you, what are the riches of his glorious inheritance in the saints, and what is the immeasurable greatness of his power in us who believe.

Fairly comprehensive! Similarly, faced with a deteriorating and theologically confused situation, he encourages Timothy to cling to Christian teaching and Old Testament Scripture, because he is convinced that in those the Christian has all he needs 'for teaching, for reproof, for correction, and for training in righteousness' (2 Timothy 3:14–17).

This teaching was not merely an academic exercise. It was the imparting of God-given truths. The unconverted person could not appreciate them, could not 'receive the gifts of the Spirit of God' for they were 'folly to him' and were 'spiritually discerned' (1 Corinthians 2:14). Even when teaching Christians, the depth of the teaching had to be adjusted to their spiritual capacity. Some were, or were like, spiritual babies, incapable of taking 'solid food', and so they had to be 'fed with milk', the simple and easily digestible truths relating to the faith (1 Corinthians 3:1f.). The mature could take wisdom, although it is not a 'wisdom of this age' but 'a secret and hidden wisdom of God' which God had revealed through his Spirit (1 Corinthians 2:6–10). Their ambition should be to progress from the simplicities of God's revelation to a deep grasp of the truth, which would be enough to enable them to teach others (Hebrews 5:11–6:3).

It was not, however, simply a matter of the intellectual grasp of certain truths. In good biblical tradition, the apostles were not interested in knowledge for its own sake, but only knowledge which brought them nearer to God and which spilled over into the practicalities of everyday life and behaviour. Paul prays for the Colossian church (Colossians 1:9f.) that they might be

> filled with the knowledge of his will in all spiritual wisdom and understanding, to lead a life worthy of the Lord, fully pleasing to him, bearing fruit in every good work and increasing in the knowledge of God.

What the Philippians had 'learned and received and heard and seen' in Paul they were to *do* (Philippians 4:9). The epistles themselves contain profound theology, but their application is always intensely practical, telling those early Christians what to do in the fellowship, the home, or the world. It was the intellectual Greek who could afford to speculate, spending his time 'in nothing except telling or hearing something new' (Acts 17:21). For the biblical saint knowledge had to be applicable to life, or it was useless.

Apparently (reading 1 Timothy 1) the false teachers traded in 'myths and endless genealogies which promote speculations rather than the divine training that is in faith' (verse 4), whereas the apostles' concern was 'love that issues from a pure heart and a good conscience and sincere faith (verse 5). The counterfeit teachers 'wandered away into vain discussion' (verse 6) and there were always plenty who were ready to listen to them, who would listen to anybody without ever arriving at a knowledge of the truth (2 Timothy 3:7). This is the other reason for what the New Testament calls 'sound' teaching (1 Timothy 1:10; 2 Timothy 1:13). Paul warns the Ephesian elders (Acts 20:29f.):

> I know that after my departure fierce wolves will come in among you, not sparing the flock; and from among your own selves will arise men speaking perverse things, to draw away disciples after them,

making the charge to take heed to themselves and to the flock all the more important.

Beneath this insistence on the truth and teaching was the conviction that the gospel was no human invention, but that it had been revealed to them by the Lord. They claimed that 'what no eye has seen, nor ear heard, nor the heart of man conceived, what God has prepared for those who love him,' God had revealed to them through the Spirit (1 Corinthians 2:9f.). Their preaching and teaching was 'according to the revelation of the mystery which was kept secret for long ages' but which had now been disclosed (Romans 16:25f.). It was not their job to invent the truth, but to pass it on as 'tradition' in the proper sense of the word, and if occasion demanded to defend it.

It is in this respect that Paul defined the church as 'the household of God, which is the church of the living God, the pillar and bulwark of the truth' (1 Timothy 3:15). It was there to support the truth, like a column taking the weight of the roof. It was there to defend the truth against error like a wall. It may be significant that the verse speaks about the church literally as '*a* pillar and bulwark...'. It is not the only support and defence that the truth has. The Spirit witnesses to the truth, as does Scripture, and these two have to do it sometimes in spite of the church.

To be able to expound and explain such God-given truth required the special God-given ability of teaching which not everyone had (1 Corinthians 12:29f.). Nor was this a task which a man took up lightly. Knowledge involves the responsibility of living in the light of it; truth requires integrity of life to exemplify it. Moreover, it is one thing to know and believe for oneself; it is quite another to influence the life and faith of another. Whereas the man with the gift is responsible for its exercise, he who teaches must remember that he is all the more answerable to God. As James advises: 'Let not many of you become teachers, my brethren, for you know that we who teach shall be judged with greater strictness.' (James 3:1.) A sobering thought!

13

OVERSIGHT

In his teaching and by his own example, Jesus set new patterns for leadership. Fallen man finds it very difficult to lead others from pure motives. Pride of place, lust for power, ambition for personal prestige are all temptations to which he is open, and we do not have to look very far in the world and in its history to see them repeatedly expressed. This appears to be what Jesus was referring to when he cautioned his ambitious disciples, 'You know that those who are supposed to rule over the Gentiles lord it over them, and their great men exercise authority over them.' (Mark 10:42.) It was this very authority which James and John had just requested for themselves, to sit, one at his right hand and one at his left, in his glory. They thought they were getting their application in before the rest, but as Jesus pointed out, that is not the way in the new order. 'It shall not be so among you,' he says, 'but whoever would be great among you must be your servant, and whoever would be first among you must be slave of all.' This was the way he went about it himself. 'The Son of man also came not to be served but to serve, and to give his life a ransom for many.' (Mark 10:35–45.)

He set them a further example when they were discussing who was the greatest in the kingdom, meaning of course, which of themselves was most important. Taking a little child, a picture of humility and simplicity, he told them that the greatest in the kingdom would be the one who humbled himself in the same way (Matthew 18:1–4). He was trying to teach them the same thing at the supper when he performed the menial task of washing their feet. 'I have given you an example,' he said, 'that you also should do as I have done to you.' (John 13:1–15.)

One of his criticisms of the Pharisees was that they tended to be led astray by their love of praise and prestige, so he warns his own disciples that they should not seek position or foster personality cults. 'You are not to be called rabbi [which was a term of respect], for you have one teacher, and you are all brethren. And call no man your father on earth [another honorific title], for you have one Father, who is in heaven. Neither be called masters, for you have one master, the Christ.' Once again he concludes that the greatest must be the servant, and that it is the man who humbles himself and refuses to seek power and position whom God exalts (Matthew 23:1–12).

We find the early church re-echoing Christ's principles. Church members should 'be subject to one another out of reverence for Christ' (Ephesians 5:21) and 'through love be servants of one another' (Galatians 5:13). The word for a Christian leader which has passed into our language is just that. 'Minister' means servant, and by definition ought to exclude the self-seeking which so often spoils leadership. Unfortunately in practice it does not, and did not, always do so.

Bishops

When Paul wrote to the church at Philippi, he included in the address the 'bishops and deacons' who, we may infer, were the church officers there (Philippians 1:1). It is not the only New Testament occurrence of words like these. The first is the old translation of a word which might be better rendered 'overseer', that is, someone over the work, almost 'foreman'. (The translators of the Authorized Version had a vested interest in bishops!) We have their qualifications spelt out for us later (1 Timothy 3:1–7) in a fairly demanding profile:

above reproach, the husband of one wife [at one time], temperate, sensible, dignified, hospitable, an apt teacher, no drunkard, not violent but gentle, not quarrelsome, and no lover of money. He must manage his own household well.... He must not be a recent convert ... he must be well thought of by outsiders.

There is a great deal in the argument that when we read about 'bishops', 'elders' and 'pastors' we are reading about the same office. ('Elder' appears to refer to leadership potential rather than age.) When Paul wrote to Titus whom he left in Crete to 'appoint elders in every town', he says in the same breath that 'a bishop, as God's steward, must be blameless', giving him a list of qualifications very similar to those which he gave to Timothy (Titus 1:5–9). The third part of our equation is supplied in Paul's speech to the Ephesian elders (Acts 20:17) who were told to look after the flock over which the Holy Spirit had made them 'overseers' (Acts 20:28, translated 'guardians' in the RSV) which is the same word translated elsewhere as 'bishops'. Peter speaks in similar terms, calling upon the elders to pastor the flock (1 Peter 5:1–2), so it looks as though the overseer or bishop was the elder who was the pastor.

In New Testament times there were more than one of these officers in each local fellowship. There were 'bishops' at Philippi (Philippians 1:1), and 'elders' at Ephesus (Acts 20:17). Although the teaching gift is stressed, not everyone taught. Paul speaks about elders who rule well, 'especially those who labour in preaching and teaching' (1 Timothy 5:17), implying that some did not. All, however, had a share in the running and pastoring of the church, and the members were responsible for following their lead. 'Obey your leaders and submit to them,' the Hebrew Christians were told (Hebrews 13:17), 'for they are keeping watch over your souls, as men who will have to give account. Let them do this joyfully, and not sadly, for that would be of no advantage to you.'

As we have seen, there were elders early on at Jerusalem working alongside the apostles (Acts 11:30; 15:6), and Paul

provided for the leadership of the new churches in Asia Minor
in the same way. In his absence, delegates like Timothy and
Titus did the same work (Titus 1:5; 1 Timothy 3:1–7). We
have no record of the beginning of this practice, but it may be
that Jewish Christians, raised in the atmosphere of a
synagogue with its officers, were led to think in similar terms
about their new assemblies.

One of the historical problems attaching to this subject
is that, shortly after the New Testament era, in the early
second century, we find a certain Ignatius writing in the
strongest terms about one bishop per church who had fairly
wide powers. Some have suggested that this singularity
derived from the apostles, that is, that the bishops were their
successors and replaced them as the apostles died out. This
is hardly likely as we find both these offices functioning
together in the New Testament. Perhaps a better pattern of
development might be, as some suggest, the 'chairman'
of the group being singled out from the plural oversight as
overall leader. In the last analysis, however, we do not know.

Deacons

The other office mentioned at Philippi is that of deacon or
'servant', some would even suggest 'table waiter' (Philippians
1:1). This word is sometimes translated 'minister' and used
in a more general sense. Paul tells us that, in God's purpose,
he became a minister of the church, although he was commissioned as an apostle (Colossians 1:25). It seems to have
a narrower, more technical sense, for Paul gives a list of
qualifications for this job too: 'serious, not double-tongued,
not addicted to much wine, not greedy for gain', with a clear
conscience, having been proved as above reproach and with
good domestic relationships (1 Timothy 3:8–13). We have
no indication of what they actually did, unless the Seven
appointed in the early days at Jerusalem were the prototype
deacons. They were elected to oversee the practical adminis-
tration of things like the common fund for the poor, so

that the apostles could get on with 'prayer and ... the ministry of the word' (Acts 6:1–6). They are not actually called 'deacons' but the same root is used in the apostles' assertion, 'It is not right that we should give up preaching the word of God to serve tables.' (Acts 6:2.)

It must not be concluded that these officers were to be of lesser spiritual stature because their duties were administrative. Their qualifications included being 'full of the Spirit and of wisdom', and their activities included miracle working and preaching in the case of Stephen (Acts 6:8–10) and evangelism in the case of Philip (Acts 8:4–13). It also appears that there were women deacons. Phoebe is described as serving the church at Cenchreae in this capacity (Romans 16:1), and it is highly likely that they are mentioned in Paul's description when he wrote to Timothy. The phrase 'the women likewise' (1 Timothy 3:11) has often been taken as referring to deacons' wives, although it could just as readily refer to women deacons. (There are no requirements for the wives of bishops in the same way.) If so, they were to be women of spiritual stature, 'serious, no slanderers, but temperate, faithful in all things'.

The place of women

The part played by women in the ministry and oversight of the church is much debated. For some the case is quite clear: Paul forbids it. He tells the women at Corinth to keep quiet in public assembly. 'They are not permitted to speak, but should be subordinate, as even the law says.... For it is shameful for a woman to speak in church.' (1 Corinthians 14:34–35.) He will not allow Timothy to admit them to a teaching or leadership position. They are to keep silent, and the reason he gives is that Adam was formed first, and Eve was deceived (1 Timothy 2:11–15).

However, the situation is not quite as unambiguous as this. In that same Corinthian situation, Paul also speaks about women praying and prophesying, and the most natural setting is that of a public meeting (1 Corinthians 11:5). He can also thank God for women who had laboured side by side with him in evangelism (Philippians 4:3). On another occasion he argues that in Christ there is no difference in status between men and women (Galatians 3:28).

These considerations have led some to argue that we must re-open the question, and ask if there are any other ways of understanding Paul's prohibitions. It could be that they were necessary in a situation where women, previously suppressed and ignorant had, in fact, been given a new status and liberty which they did not know how to handle. When Paul says, 'Let a woman learn in silence with all submissiveness,' the accent may fall on *learn* (1 Timothy 2:11). Their contribution both disrupted the church gathering (which is the main issue in 1 Corinthians 14) and embarrassed their husbands. Hence the advice, 'If there is anything they desire to know, let them ask their husbands at home,' and one might translate the rest, 'for it is a shameful thing for a woman *to chatter* in the assembly' (1 Corinthians 14:35). Elsewhere older women in particular are told to teach, although their subjects are the younger women (Titus 2:3–4), and Paul reminds Timothy that, as a child, he owed a great debt to his own mother and her teaching (2 Timothy 1:5; 3:14–15).

It is equally possible to argue that the gift qualifies for office and ministry, and not just sex. The Spirit is sovereign when it comes to distributing gifts within the fellowship (1 Corinthians 12:11), and it is unquestionable that he has on occasion gifted women in these ways. We have both the testimony of the Old Testament and church history as evidence for this. If God so gifts, who is man to argue?

It must be noted that, just as it took time for western society to come to terms with the injustice of slavery, the equality of women has also been a long time coming, and yet Paul himself elaborates the principle which justifies both these developments. In Christ, he says, 'there is neither slave nor free, there is neither male nor female' (Galatians 3:28).

At the same time Scripture never understands women as men with a different shape! Both men and women were so created that they have complementary roles to play. This comes out most strongly where we would expect it, in the biblical view of marriage. There it is clear that man is so constituted that he must take a lead. 'The head of every man is Christ, the head of a woman is her husband.' (1 Corinthians 11:3.) As far as Scripture is concerned, this is not just the role imposed on woman by society. It has its basis in the way in which men and women were made in the first place. 'Adam was formed first, then Eve.' (1 Timothy 2:13.) This does not reduce the woman to insignificance, but it does mean that when it comes to leadership in the church, a man's psychological make-up might better qualify him without excluding her. Paul's words against women having authority over men might be translated as 'lording it over them' or even laying down the law to men in public (1 Timothy 2:12). The whole issue is complicated by Paul's assumption in the passages quoted that the women in question are married, and he could be dealing with their attitude to their husbands in the meetings rather than with general principles.

The ministry

Ministers are never called 'priests' in the New Testament. The office of priest as one who stands between God and man, or one who offers sacrifices on behalf of man, has been swallowed up once and for all in Christ and what he has done. This is the theme of the epistle to the Hebrews. Because of our new freedom of access into God's presence through Christ, *all* are described as priests (1 Peter 2:5, 9; Revelation 1:6; 5:10; 20:6), and the service that we render must now be that of 'spiritual sacrifices acceptable to God through Jesus Christ'. This is what has traditionally been called 'the priesthood of all believers'.

Were the New Testament ministers paid? Paul makes it quite clear that they ought to be. He uses various arguments to establish that 'those who proclaim the gospel should get their living by the gospel' (1 Corinthians 9:3–14). As we have seen, he himself refused support so that no one could accuse him of preaching for what he could make out of it. In normal circumstances it was simply an expression of fellowship. He may be talking about the same thing when he tells Timothy, 'Let the elders who rule well be considered worthy of double honour, especially those who labour in preaching and teaching.' (1 Timothy 5:17.) Some would translate it 'double stipend'!

Whereas there are a good number of Bible promises of God's supply, the only instance of the modern principle of 'living by faith' is connected with the mission on which Jesus sent his disciples. They were told, 'Take no gold, nor silver, nor copper in your belts, no bag for your journey, nor two tunics, nor sandals, nor a staff,' (Matthew 10:9–10). A similar principle is applied even there, 'for the labourer deserves his food'. We must remember that travellers could expect short-term hospitality in that culture. It is perhaps significant that, when Paul ran short of funds, he did not 'live by faith' in the modern sense, but took up his old trade to earn his keep, even though it meant labouring 'night and day' (Acts 18:1–4; 1 Thessalonians 2:9; 2 Thessalonians 3:7–10). God may well call some to live in simple dependence on him without even making their needs known to others, but the regular principle for the support of workers in the New Testament churches was not that way.

'Ordination' in the modern sense of the term is not found in the New Testament, but we do have the recognition of men who were to exercise a particular function in the church. The Seven at Jerusalem, having been chosen by the church members, were set apart with prayer and the laying on of hands (Acts 6:6). Similarly Paul and Barnabas were commissioned publicly for their first missionary journey, although in that case the church was simply endorsing what the Holy Spirit had already made clear: 'The Holy Spirit said, "Set apart for me Barnabas and Saul" ... Then after fasting and prayer they laid their hands on them and sent them off.' (Acts 13:2–3.)

The laying on of hands does not always mean ordination (if we are to use that word), as it was equally employed in actions like the gifting of the Spirit (Acts 8:17) or healing (Luke 4:40). It is an Old Testament practice, and seems to have the essential meaning of identification. In the case of ministry, it could be that the church is identifying itself with the person concerned in their God-given call and office. Timothy is warned not to lay hands on anyone with undue haste (1 Timothy 5:22). Perhaps there had been a breakdown in the system and some had been set apart for ministry without either the necessary gifts or character. In the appointment of overseers, the candidate 'must not be a recent convert, or he may be puffed up with conceit and fall into the condemnation of the devil' (1 Timothy 3:6). Youth in itself was apparently not necessarily a bar to office. Timothy had that problem himself, and yet he had been commissioned to the work. Paul had to remind him (1 Timothy 4:14, 12):

> Do not neglect the gift you have, which was given you by prophetic utterance when the elders laid their hands upon you. . . . Let no one despise your youth, but set the believers an example in speech and conduct, in love, in faith, in purity.

Once again, the minister is expected to live out the message that he preaches.

14

THE CHURCH AT WORSHIP

While stressing the need for private piety between worshipper and God alone (Matthew 6:1–18) and often practising it himself, Jesus also set the example of corporate worship. When he returned to the north after his baptism, on the sabbath he went to the synagogue 'as his custom was' (Luke 4:16), and we have more references to his ministry in the setting of otherwise regular synagogue services (Matthew 4:23; 9:35; 12:9; 13:54). He protested at his arrest that his preaching had been in such public places, as well as in the confines of the Temple where he attended feasts on several occasions (John 18:20). Even though he drew great crowds, in terms of ordinary Jewish religious life he was no separatist, although he did foresee the time when his followers would not be tolerated but would be 'beaten in synagogues' (Mark 13:9).

We have no record of Jesus praying *with* his disciples, but we do have the account (Matthew 6:9–13) of his teaching of the Family Prayer (the Lord's Prayer). 'Our Father' is a corporate expression. We have it on record that they sang a hymn together (Matthew 26:30), probably as part of the Passover celebration, and of course we have the institution of the corporate meal which we know as the Lord's Supper. More of that later.

It is in the early church that we find a new blossoming of worship, particularly after the coming of the Spirit at Pentecost. It is often overlooked that the phenomenon of tongues on that day was not for evangelism but praise. The mixed multitude could hear them telling in their own tongues 'the mighty works of God' (Acts 2:11). The first summary account of the activities of the young church speaks of a similar accent on praise (Acts 2:46f.).

Just as Israel of old had expressed its worship in song, the new Israel did the same. Paul encourages his friends to minister to one another in 'psalms, hymns and spiritual songs' (Ephesians 5:19; Colossians 3:16), sounding the note of praise and gratitude to God. We find him along with Silas doing just that in the most uncongenial setting of the jail at Philippi. At about midnight they 'were praying and singing hymns to God' (Acts 16:25), much to the interest of the other prisoners.

Worship was the prime purpose of the church. Christians were destined to be God's sons 'to the praise of his glorious grace', and appointed 'to live for the praise of his glory' (Ephesians 1:6, 12). They were to give back to God something of the praise and adoration which was his due, 'the fruit of lips that acknowledge his name' (Hebrew 13:15). Because of the ministry of the Spirit, it was an activity in which they could engage without the structure of priest and Temple, 'in spirit and truth' as Jesus had predicted (John 4:21–24). Such, according to Paul, are the true people of God 'who worship God in spirit' (Philippians 3:3). All had been fulfilled in Christ, and each believer could come freely and confidently to God (Hebrews 4:16).

It may be the case that we have examples of their early hymns embedded in the New Testament letters. For a variety of reasons, some scholars suspect that Philippians 2:5–11 or Colossians 1:15–20 might have first been sung within the fellowship. If this is the case, the Lord Jesus Christ in his risen, ascended glory formed the main theme of their praise. Others have suspected that the profound statements of worship in the book of Revelation might reflect something of the worship times of the church, even though they are set in heaven.

From the very beginning the disciples engaged in corporate

prayer. Even before the Spirit came, they prayed together (Acts 1:14, 24f.), and after he did the pattern continued with greater fervour. 'They devoted themselves to ... the prayers' (Acts 2:42, which may refer to prayers in the Temple). After their defence to the Council, Peter and John went back to a prayer meeting (Acts 4:23–31), and when Peter was imprisoned 'earnest prayer for him was made to God by the church' (Acts 12:5).

Paul asks for and exhorts to prayer. They are to strive together in their prayers for him at Rome (Romans 15:30). He is confident that the prayers of the Philippians will play a part in his deliverance (Philippians 1:19), while he particularly requests prayer of the Ephesians that he might preach boldly (Ephesians 6:18f.). When informing Timothy of his duties at Ephesus, 'supplications, prayers, intercessions, and thanksgivings ... for all men, for kings and all who are in high positions' come at the top of the list (1 Timothy 2:1f.). They must be concerned with wider issues than their own local affairs.

James outlines the proper expression for differing spiritual conditions. Those suffering should pray. Those cheerful should praise, and those who were sick should request special prayer and anointing from the hands of the church officers (James 5:13–16).

In correcting the chaos at Corinth, Paul incidentally gives us an insight into the way their services were run (1 Corinthians 14). His argument with the church was over the misuse of the gift of tongues, a gift which he does not deny, but which he severely disciplines. Worship was to be a shared experience. All could make some contribution, whether it be 'a hymn, a lesson, a revelation, a tongue, or an interpretation' (verse 26), but not without discipline and order. 'God is not a God of confusion but of peace,' he says (verse 33). In his mind, the keynote was the upbuilding of Christians in their faith, and this was his basis for limiting the use of the gift of tongues. His rule in summary was 'no tongues without an interpreter', and 'no more than two or three in each service'. Paul puts far greater emphasis on prophecy, simply because everyone could understand what was being said and no one was left out. The gift of tongues could be of great private blessing. Even with prophecy, however, a man's words came under scrutiny. The others should 'weigh what is said' (verse 29) and no one was allowed to minister when another had the floor (verse 27).

We have an interesting side-glance at the congregation, too, because Paul not only mentions believers, but also 'outsiders and unbelievers'. The service is manifestly a worship service, and yet the possibility of the unconverted being present is not ruled out. On the contrary, it could lead to their conversion.

At Corinth they were also troubled by irreverent behaviour on the part of the women (1 Corinthians 11:2–16). Here we are at the disadvantage of not being able to reconstruct the original circumstances, and the words themselves are not entirely clear. Many have traditionally understood the passage as legislating for women's headgear. The man must worship with head uncovered, the woman with some kind of head-covering. However, it is not quite as straightforward as that. There are one or two problems, the first being that a hair-covering and the length of a woman's hair meant something rather different in that society from our own. It was disgraceful for her either to go hatless – some would say, without a veil (although the word does not occur) – or to have short hair. Either way she would shame her husband. If this is no longer so, the argument seems to have lost its point.

However, there is also the difficulty of understanding Paul's reason for his legislation: literally 'a woman ought to have authority on her head, because of the angels' (verse 10). In what way is a head-covering authority? Some have suggested that the head-covering gave a woman freedom of movement in public, just as a veil does in some parts of the world today, while the uncovered woman was the immoral one. So the authority might be her new found independence in Christ. Are the angels lustful or offended bystanders in

Christian worship? Or does the word refer to the preachers who might be distracted by the attractive members of the congregation? It is all rather obscure.

When did the church meet for worship? In the early days at Jerusalem they could not meet often enough, either in the Temple, or in one another's homes (Acts 2:46). While still operating in the synagogues, they met on the sabbath day (Acts 13:14, 44). By the time of Paul's third missionary journey, it was evidently the practice to meet to break bread 'on the first day of the week' (Acts 20:7), and at Corinth they were told to make their offering for the collection on that day (1 Corinthians 16:2). This probably came to be known as 'the Lord's day' (Revelation 1:10), to be distinguished from 'the day of the Lord' in the sense of Judgement Day. No reason is given for this, but the Lord's appearing to his disciples on the first day of the week most likely made them come with anticipation on that day for worship, and to remember him till he should return. For most, of course, it would have been an ordinary working day, and they would have to meet early or in the evening. It seems that at Troas the evening meeting went on past midnight when Paul preached to them (Acts 20:7).

The eager and spontaneous worship pictured for us in books like Acts or 1 Corinthians was unfortunately not always in evidence. Some actually had to be reminded not to neglect the meetings, and to exhort and encourage one another (Hebrews 10:25). Others used the gathering as an occasion for ostentation (James 2:2–3) or even gluttony and drunkenness (1 Corinthians 11:21), but it was their abuse which, in the providence of God, gives us an insight into their worship which we should never otherwise have had.

15

THE LORD'S SUPPER

One of the last things which Jesus did with his disciples before he went to the cross was to host a common meal which was to be the forerunner of what we call 'the Lord's Supper' or 'Holy Communion'. There are slight variations in the gospel accounts (Matthew 26:26–29; Mark 14:22–25; Luke 22:17–20), and we owe to Paul the record of Christ's command to do it in remembrance of him (1 Corinthians 11:23–26). In summary, Jesus took bread and having given thanks ('blessed' means the same thing – God is blessed for his gift) he broke it and said, 'Take and eat; this is my body which is given [or broken] for you. Do this in remembrance of me.' After supper he took the cup and gave thanks and said, 'Drink of this, all of you [or 'Divide it among yourselves']; this is my blood of the covenant [or my blood of the new covenant] which is shed for many for the forgiveness of sins. Do this in remembrance of me.'

Because of this, eating together became an established part of church life from the beginning. Those who received Peter's word at Pentecost devoted themselves 'to the breaking of bread' among other things (Acts 2:42). 'Day by day ... they partook of food with glad and generous hearts.' (Acts 2:46.) By the time of Paul's third missionary journey, it seems to have become a regular Sunday practice. At Troas, on the first day of the week, they were 'gathered together to break bread' (Acts 20:7), remembering Christ in his own appointed way.

The Passover and the New Covenant

The word 'remembrance' means more than simply 'calling to mind'. It probably has the Jewish idea behind it of re-enacting the event, just in the same way that they re-enacted the Passover meal each year. It was as though each generation had come out of Egypt with the original number. Christ's death was seen in Passover terms. Paul wrote that 'Christ, our paschal lamb, has been sacrificed,' and he used the imagery of clearing the house of leaven, a regular practice at Passover time, to speak of ridding ourselves of evil (1 Corinthians 5:6–8). This may be because the original supper was part of the Passover meal (Matthew 26:17).

The Passover supper was, and is, part service, part festive meal. There were four cups of wine, two before the meal and two in the conclusion to the celebration, during which a portion of unleavened bread, kept from the first part, was broken and shared among the guests. There have been various reconstructions, but the most plausible seems to be that which makes 'the Lord's Supper' take place in this conclusion. This may account for the rather strange order of Luke's account with a cup *before* the bread and, some authorities add, a cup afterwards as well. It might also explain Paul's reference to 'after supper' (1 Corinthians 11:25). If this is so, Jesus is taking the Passover ritual and filling it with new meaning centring on his death. Other scholars have compared the original supper with the common meals which rabbis used to hold with their disciples on Friday evenings.

Certainly Jesus filled the simple act of eating and drinking with profound significance. The broken bread and the out-poured wine spoke vividly of his impending death the following day. The words that he used had even greater significance for his Jewish listeners than they would have had for us, for the phrase 'my blood of the [new] covenant' links together two well-known Old Testament themes. At the first covenant making, Moses had offered sacrifice, sprinkling the blood on the people, and declaring it to be 'the blood of the covenant' which God had made with them that day (Exodus 24:8).

Later in their history, Jeremiah had been given the vision of a new covenant which would replace the old, with which went the promise of forgiven sins (Jeremiah 31:31–34). Jesus is now claiming that this New Covenant was about to be ratified and brought into existence by his death. Their eating and drinking spoke of their sharing in the benefits.

The meaning of the Communion

John has no account of the supper in his gospel, but he does record a most interesting discourse after the feeding of the five thousand (John 6:25–65). Comparing himself with the manna which God had given the children of Israel in their desert wanderings, Jesus claims to be 'the bread of life'. He goes on to speak of this bread as his flesh which he would give for the world, an idea which the Jews found repulsive. Jesus' own explanation was to point out that he was not advocating literal cannibalism, but that the meaning of his words were 'spirit and life'. We need to take what Christ has done for ourselves, and the Lord's Supper represents our sharing in the benefits of his death.

It is sad to think that Paul's description of the Supper only comes down to us because of the abuse of this meal in the Corinthian church (1 Corinthians 11:17–34). It is not the only time that Christians are recorded as coming unworthily to the Lord's table. Jude speaks of some false teachers as 'blemishes on your love feasts' (Jude 12; 2 Peter 2:13 might carry the same meaning). The whole force of Paul's teaching on the subject is that one cannot come to the meal lightly, or it ceases to be the Lord's Supper. Earlier in the letter he warned the Corinthians about their spiritual complacency by suggesting a parallel between baptism and the Lord's Supper and the wilderness experiences of God's Old Covenant people. Even attendance at a Communion service was no guarantee of spiritual security (1 Corinthians 10:1–5).

It seems that the Communion was originally part of a common

church meal, or 'love feast', to which individual members brought their own contribution. Unfortunately at Corinth the Christians had entirely missed the spirit of the gathering, and instead of an expression of love, it had become an occasion for selfishness. Some had little and went hungry. Others brought a great deal and over-ate – and over-drank, so that some were even drunk when it came to the breaking of bread. There was no thought of sharing; in fact they were deeply divided. The meal had become a contradiction in terms and calls out Paul's sharp rebuke together with instruction as to how to conduct themselves.

There are interesting features in the account which give further clues as to the meaning of the Communion itself. Paul first of all describes the action as a proclamation of the Lord's death. This does not mean that it was an evangelistic occasion. In a sense they were preaching to themselves as they 'acted out' the Supper. The very broken bread and outpoured wine visibly 'proclaimed' the crucifixion to those taking part. It might have reference to preaching ministry accompanying the meal, just in the same way that the Passover was accompanied by a statement of the meaning of the event.

It is also interesting to note that Paul's institution account, like those of the gospels, has reference to the future consummation of Christ's work at his return. They were to do it 'until he comes'. As well as pointing back to Calvary, the Communion service looks forward to the blessedness of the age to come. It may be no coincidence that the Jews often pictured this happy condition in terms of the Messiah's banquet to which they would be invited.

Perhaps the most difficult aspect to understand is the little phrase 'discerning the body'. It was their failure to do this which had, in Paul's opinion, brought sickness and even death on some of the Corinthian members. Some feel that it is a technical way of describing desecration. It was like a personal offence against Christ himself. Others have suggested that there was something in the bread and wine that needed careful handling. If not it would get out and do damage, rather like high tension electricity. An alternative idea is that their behaviour at the supper had the effect of hindering the miraculous healing ministry of the church. That is, sickness and death were not directly caused by their mishandling of the bread and wine, but ran their course unchecked. Some have suggested that Paul's reference to the body is a reference to the church, that is, their behaviour was 'despising the church of God' as he says.

In terms of modern understanding, this phrase has been widely interpreted from the extreme of sacramentalism, which maintains that the bread and wine become the actual body and blood of Christ, to that where the whole meal is merely symbolical, a simple momento of Christ's death. However, there is surely something special about the supper which makes it more than a mere symbol. After all, a good number of things might serve to remind us of Christ's death, but this was the way in which he himself especially intended it to be so. Perhaps we might take the old analogy of the word of God. Just as God uses Scripture in a special way, in a way in which he uses no other book, to save men and women, so he uses this special memorial meal to bless them. He has chosen this occasion to be particularly present and to be made known to his friends in the breaking of bread.

Sometimes these days we hear the Lord's Supper being called 'the Eucharist'. This is not just a 'high church' way of putting it, as the word simply means 'thanksgiving'. It goes back to the grace which Jesus said at the original supper when he gave thanks and then broke the bread.

Another aspect of the service comes out quite incidentally in the same letter (1 Corinthians 10:14–22). Paul was dealing with a problem we have already mentioned, that of whether or not Christians were free to attend meals in idol temples or to eat meat which had been offered to idols. This was a real issue, of course, when most pagan dinner parties would take place in this setting. Either they had to turn a blind eye to it, or they had to cut themselves off from a good number of their non-Christian friends and their society. Some Corinthians decided that as they were above all scruples, it did not matter either way. Paul tells them that their eating symbolizes something more profound than they had imagined.

For him, eating meant fellowship. It was so in the Jewish Temple, and it was so in the Lord's Supper. The meal is a fellowship meal, a Communion, an expression of the oneness of the whole church with one another and with Christ. Idol sacrifice-meals were similar. They brought those who partook not only into fellowship with one another in a social way, but into fellowship with the demons who stood behind idol worship, something utterly inconsistent with their fellowship with Christ. So their practice might even provoke the Lord to jealousy and open them to judgement. What is important for us, however, is the positive side. As we have said, fellowship is two-way. The meal represents our fellowship with one another, and that we can readily appreciate, but it also, if rightly observed, brings us into close fellowship with Christ himself. To use Paul's word, it is a 'participation' in the body and blood of Christ.

16

THE CHURCH IN THE WORLD

Although Christians were God's pilgrim people whose citizenship was in heaven, they still had to live in this world and come to terms with its institutions. The very term 'world' often has a sinister ring in the New Testament, as it was used there not only of ordered creation, or the world of people, but more specifically of the world of fallen, sinful men and women. When praying for his friends, Jesus said (John 17:14f.):

> I have given them thy word; and the world has hated them because they are not of the world, even as I am not of the world. I do not pray that thou shouldst take them out of the world, but that thou shouldst keep them from the evil one.

A similar term is 'age'. The Jews divided time between this present age and the age to come, the Messiah's age. The message of the gospel was that the Messiah had come, and therefore the age to come must have come too. Putting our trust in Christ, we become 'partakers of the Holy Spirit', having 'tasted the goodness of the word of God and the powers of the age to come' (Hebrews 6:4f.). We are already living in the new age. 'Eternal life' means literally 'life of the age'. There has been an overlap of two distinct ages in our experience, for the present, evil age will continue until Christ returns, and this means that we are living in a tension between the two.

This present world age is under the authority of Satan, 'the god of this world' (2 Corinthians 4:4). Christians have been delivered from the 'dominion of darkness' and transferred to the kingdom of Christ (Colossians 1:13). Hence there must be conflict between the attitudes, values, standards and outlook of this present world and those of the Christian. 'The form of this world is passing away' (1 Corinthians 7:31), but in the meantime the Christian's life-style and that of those among whom he lives will often contradict one another.

In this sense, there can be no truck with the world, as it represents the very antithesis of the Christian's new profession at so many points. John warns his readers (1 John 2:15–17):

> Do not love the world or the things in the world. If any one loves the world, love for the Father is not in him. For all that is in the world, the lust of the flesh and the lust of the eyes and the pride of life, is not of the Father but is of the world. And the world passes away, and the lust of it.

It was this world, 'the rulers of this world', who had crucified their Lord (1 Corinthians 2:8), and who would deal out similar treatment to his followers. It is therefore seen in alien terms, a power to overcome. 'Whatever is born of God overcomes the world; and this is the victory that overcomes the world, our faith.' (1 John 5:4.)

As we have seen, this called for a separation on the part of the church. A worldly church, that is, a group of Christians living like the rest, have nothing to offer. However, the apostles did not found convents and monasteries. Their understanding of things allowed them to live in the world without becoming a part of it. One area with which they had to come to terms was that of the human institutions of their day.

Under authority

We have already seen that their legal position changed as time went by. Initially regarded as a Jewish sect, they were not opposed by the authorities, at least not outside Palestine. When the church became more obviously a Gentile movement as well, the authorities began to take an interest which in greater or lesser degree resulted in persecution for the first three hundred years of church history.

Jesus himself set the example of respect for constituted authorities. He paid the tax with the coin from the fish's mouth, although he pointed out to Peter that he had no need to, and that he did it 'not to give offence to them' (Matthew 17:24–27). Although 'the sons are free' they ought voluntarily to submit to the rules. He also carefully skirted the politically loaded question about taxes, by saying in effect that we have responsibilities both to God and to the constituted authorities. 'Render therefore to Caesar the things that are Caesar's, and to God the things that are God's.' (Matthew 22:15–22.) Although he was crucified on a political charge, there is nothing in his teaching which could be interpreted as political revolution, a fact that Pilate himself acknowledged (John 18:33–38).

We find the same respect for the authorities in Paul's writings. He regarded earthly rulers as being part of the divinely appointed restraint upon the evil of man, and therefore deserving honour. To resist them would be to resist God. In so far as they promote what is good, rulers are God's servants, although perhaps unwittingly. So they must pay all their dues, taxes, respect and honour when they are called for (Romans 13:1–7). As we have noted, he commanded Timothy to pray for the authorities 'that we may lead a quiet and peaceable life, godly and respectful in every way' (1 Timothy 2:1–3). 'This is good, and it is acceptable in the sight of God our Saviour,' whose concern, says Paul, is that all men might be saved. If that is so, rebellion or civil disobedience would not help the spread of the gospel but rather prejudice men against it. He himself tried to cultivate a healthy relationship with the Roman authorities. He had great influence on Sergius Paulus, the proconsul in Cyprus (Acts 13:7–12), and when Gallio was proconsul of Achaia, he took Paul's part (Acts 18:12–17). On occasion he used the fact that he was a Roman citizen, and therefore possessing certain rights, to get him out of difficulties (Acts 16:37–39; 22:22–29). His relationship with the procurators Felix and Festus seems to have been a friendly one, and we finally see him travelling to Rome at the expense of the state.

We find a similar respect for the social structure of the time. Even slavery is not condemned, although in terms of Christian fellowship there were principles which would eventually undermine it. There is no hint anywhere that, for all their pessimistic assessment of 'this world', the apostles were set on political revolution, or even on social change. Being a minority group under a dictatorship this did not become their concern. Their ambition was to preach the gospel and see the church grow, a process which eventually had a revolutionary effect on society, but not in the usual sense.

Against authority

What happened when conflict was inevitable? How did they react when Caesar claimed what belonged to God? The answer is simply that their allegiance to Christ came first. When Peter and John were warned in the early days that they must not speak any more in the name of Christ, they replied, 'Whether it is right in the sight of God to listen to you rather than to God, you must judge; for we cannot but speak of what we have seen and heard.' (Acts 4:18–20.) Then they went out and continued to make Christ known. It meant, of course, taking the consequences. It meant imprisonment, beating, and even (as in Stephen's case) martyrdom.

Persecution is a frequent New Testament theme, although it did not always come from official sources. There were occasions when the mob took the law into their own hands, as they did at Ephesus (Acts 19:23–41). We may have official opposition reflected in Peter's writing. He speaks about suffering 'as a Christian' and tries to stiffen his friends in the time of tribulation which was coming their way (1 Peter 4:12f.):

Do not be surprised at the fiery ordeal which comes upon you to prove you, as though something strange were happening to you. But rejoice in so far as you share Christ's sufferings, that you may also rejoice and be glad when his glory is revealed.

Once detached from Judaism, being a Christian would be

illegal, and therefore a believer was fair game for any informer, depending on the zeal of the provincial governor or judge. By the time we get to Revelation, we find John exiled on Patmos 'on account of the word of God and the testimony of Jesus' (Revelation 1:9), and the Roman authorities thinly disguised in many of the harsher symbols of the book.

All this meant that life could often be extremely insecure for a first-century Christian. This fact may stand behind Paul's advice about marriage and many of the other commitments of life. He talks about 'the impending [or present] distress' and suggests that they would be better not to marry, perhaps because they would be less vulnerable if they remained single. Similarly, 'the appointed time' had grown very short. 'The form of this world is passing away,' and this would influence their domestic and business affairs (1 Corinthians 7:25–31).

One gets the impression that, as far as life-style is concerned, the Christian ought to be 'travelling light'. He does not really belong here. He acknowledges that he is a stranger and a pilgrim on earth, seeking another homeland (Hebrews 11:13–16). His deepest longings and ambitions, given by an indwelling Holy Spirit, can never be fulfilled in this world. They will only be satisfied in glory.

17

MISSION

While having a very clear sense of its own identity over against the world, the New Testament church was in no way introverted or even defensive. On the contrary, the record of the book of Acts is one of an aggressive advance into what was previously Satan's domain, often with the Lord adding daily to the number.

Before Jesus

In this respect the church stood in sharp contrast to the nation of Israel, though in this way it was fulfilling part of Israel's destiny and purpose. We have seen that God's dealings with Israel were in order that every family of the earth should ultimately be blessed, and this was a constantly repeated theme with the Old Testament prophets. Isaiah in particular had a clear vision that one day God would bless the world through Israel (Isaiah 2:2f.):

> It shall come to pass in the latter days that the mountain of the house of the LORD shall be established as the highest of the mountains, and shall be raised above the hills; and all the nations shall flow to it, and many peoples shall come, and say: 'Come, let us go up to the mountain of the LORD, to the house of the God of Jacob; that he may teach us his ways and that we may walk in his paths.'

The appeal goes out through the 'evangelical prophet', 'Turn to me and be saved, all the ends of the earth!' (Isaiah 45:22).

God's servant would be 'a light to the nations, that my salvation may reach to the end of the earth' (Isaiah 49:6). God's house would be called 'a house of prayer for all peoples' (Isaiah 56:7). Similarly Jeremiah and others foresaw the day when all the nations would come and share the blessings of Israel.

This was not easy even for Old Testament Jews to take. The book of Jonah may well be asking the question, 'How can God forgive the wicked?' and by the time of Jesus these predictions left some Jews with an uneasy conscience as far as the Gentiles were concerned. There had been a sort of missionary expansion during the period between the Testaments, although it was mostly compulsory proselytism by force of conquest. This is how Herod the Great's family, Idumaean or Edomite by line, could rule over the Jews. Jesus mentioned the Pharisees' zeal in making converts: 'you traverse sea and land to make a single proselyte, and when he becomes a proselyte, you make him twice as much a child of hell as yourselves' (Matthew 23:15). Perhaps the most productive field was the synagogue set in a non-Jewish town or city where Gentiles were welcome to attend and listen. These attracted a good number who, even if they did not become full Jews, were so committed to the Jewish faith that they were known as 'God-fearers', a group who were always very responsive to the gospel message when Paul and his like preached it in the synagogues. By and large, however, Gentiles were beyond the pale, untouchable, dogs, unclean. It took the love of Christ and the compulsion of the Holy Spirit to break down the barriers.

In the time of Jesus

Jesus himself came with a sense of mission, that is, of being sent. The Father had sent him, and he had come into the world to rescue those who were lost, after seeking them out (Luke 19:10). One of the distinctive features of Jesus' teaching was that God did not wait for men and women to turn to him, but that rather he took the initiative and made the first move towards them. Jesus came calling sinful men and women to repentance and faith, as well as making a way back to God for them through his death. Although he professedly confined his ministry to 'the lost sheep of the house of Israel', his compassion overflowed to those outside the scope of that job description. He healed the centurion's servant, marvelling at his faith as a Gentile (Matthew 8:5–13). He also helped the Canaanite woman when he saw that her faith was great enough (Matthew 15:21–28). In so doing he anticipated the vast expansion of the gospel to the Gentiles.

During his ministry Jesus also sent his disciples out to preach and to heal, first the Twelve (Matthew 10) and then a further seventy (Luke 10:1–20). Their commissioning was similar. They went with delegated authority to prepare the way for himself. They were to travel light and fast. They were to present their offer on a 'take it or leave it' basis. They were to confine their attentions to the Jews.

Jesus told them that 'the harvest is plentiful, but the labourers are few', and that they must pray for more (Matthew 9:37–38). He also dropped hints that, in the future, the response would be far wider than anything they had seen. At the last Passover, some Gentiles requested to see Jesus, and when he heard he responded (John 12:24, 31–32):

> Truly, truly, I say to you, unless a grain of wheat falls into the earth and dies, it remains alone; but if it dies, it bears much fruit. . . . Now is the judgment of this world, now shall the ruler of this world be cast out; and I, when I am lifted up from the earth, will draw all men to myself.

When describing the end times to his disciples, he tells them that 'this gospel of the kingdom will be preached throughout the whole world, as a testimony to all nations', and when he returned his angels would 'gather his elect from the four winds, from one end of heaven to the other' (Matthew 24:14, 31).

It was after his resurrection that Jesus explicitly commanded his disciples to take the message worldwide. This was to be in fulfilment of Scripture, just like his unexpected death and resurrection, 'that repentance and forgiveness of sins should be preached in his name to all nations, beginning from Jerusalem' (Luke 24:47). It was an aspect of the lordship bestowed on him (Matthew 28:18–20):

> All authority in heaven and on earth has been given to me. Go therefore and make disciples of all nations, baptizing them in the name of the Father and of the Son and of the Holy Spirit, teaching them to observe all that I have commanded you; and lo, I am with you always, to the close of the age.

It was a similar commission to his own. 'As the Father has sent me,' he told them, 'even so I send you.' (John 20:21.) It was to be with the power of the Holy Spirit. At his ascension he promised that they would receive power when the Holy Spirit would come upon them, and then they would be witnesses in Jerusalem and in Judea and Samaria, 'and to the end of the earth' (Acts 1:8).

After Jesus

The interesting aspect of mission in the New Testament is that these are practically the only general commands to preach the gospel that we have. Paul himself was personally commissioned to the work (Acts 9:15–16; 22:21; 26:16–18). Timothy is told to do the work of an evangelist (2 Timothy 2:2). We have the odd word about witness here and there, but apart from these there are no continuing exhortations to get on with the job of spreading the gospel message. Perhaps the conclusion we are meant to draw is that they did not need commanding. They spontaneously shared Christ in such a way that the church appears to have expanded faster than at any time since.

The book of Acts is a stirring record of only part of what went on. It tells of the early days, of the effect of persecution, and then concentrates on aspects of Paul's career. We must remember that this is only a partial picture of the missionary explosion of the first century. For example, when Paul wrote to Rome, there was already a flourishing church there.

We do not know who founded it. The letter to the Colossians was written by the apostle to a church he had not visited. The seven churches of Revelation include locations not mentioned in the book of Acts. Peter can write to Christians scattered over a wide area, 'Pontus, Galatia, Cappadocia, Asia, and Bithynia' (1 Peter 1:1). Barnabas and Mark sailed away to Cyprus (Acts 15:39) and we hear little more of them, but their work doubtless went on.

The four gospels were written at an early date by Greek-speaking Christians who wanted to share their faith. They are much more than biography. They are more akin to gospel tracts designed to bring their hearers to faith in Christ. Mark starts his, 'the beginning of the gospel of Jesus Christ, the Son of God,' (Mark 1:1), and John almost ends his saying that although Jesus did many other things which he had not recorded in that book, 'these are written that you may believe that Jesus is the Christ, the Son of God, and that believing you may have life in his name' (John 20:30–31).

Acts gives us some clues to this rapid expansion. The immediate result of Pentecost was the preaching of the gospel. It was a gospel aimed at Jews and it elicited tremendous response. That the apostles conceived their task in this way is evident by the way in which they answered the accusing Jewish Council. God had raised his Son whom they had crucified. There was no other way of salvation. They could not but speak of the things which they had seen and heard, and though warned of dire consequences if they did, filled with the Spirit they continued to speak the word of God with boldness (Acts 4:8–31). It was gospel preaching backed by, and sometimes stemming from miraculous signs which were incontrovertible. A collision with the authorities was bound to come, and when it did, Stephen's testimony and martyrdom led to the scattering of the church.

It has been argued that persecution was the spur which drove the early church to evangelize beyond Jerusalem. If this were the whole story, it would have been more logical for the dispersed Christians to have kept quiet. As it was, 'those who were scattered went about preaching the word' (Acts 8:4). Our records are incomplete. The work may have been going on before the Jerusalem community was driven underground or out into the country. Philip's activity in Samaria and then with the Ethiopian official (Acts 8) are just a couple of examples of the kind of thing that was going on.

Initially confining their message to the Jews, some found a ready acceptance among Gentiles as well, especially at Antioch (Acts 11:19–21). Peter himself had already been led against his better judgement (as he thought) to see that the gospel could save non-Jews too (Acts 10:1–11:18). Barnabas, who was sent to Antioch to check the development, was thrilled by what he found, and drew Paul into the work (Acts 11:22–26).

It is tempting to ask what Paul had been doing in Tarsus, or before that in Arabia, after his conversion (Galatians 1:17). It is one of the tantalizing silences of the New Testament. We do know that he was preaching almost as soon as he was converted (Acts 9:20), and that he felt particularly burdened for the Gentiles (Acts 22:21), in itself a miracle for an orthodox Jew. Half of Acts is given over to an account of some of his work during three missionary journeys, and then his trip to Rome as a prisoner. There is some evidence that he might have been released from detainment for a further period of missionary activity before finally being put to death. He shared his plans with the Roman church to move over to the west of the empire, to Spain, after his visit to Jerusalem (Romans 15:18–29). We do not know if he ever got there.

What points stand out in the evangelism reported in Acts? It is evident that the pattern of Paul's ministry was not haphazard; it was worked out by the Spirit (Acts 16:6–10). It so happened that he visited the strategic centres of population from which the surrounding countryside could be evangelized. His personal concern was to go to places where the gospel had not been previously preached (Romans 15:20).

The preachers went out with a sense of compulsion which we also find described in the letters, a zeal which did not tire in spite of great opposition. Paul says:

Him we proclaim, warning every man and teaching every man
in all wisdom, that we may present every man mature in Christ.
For this I toil, striving with all the energy which he mightily
inspires within me. [Colossians 1:28f.]

We are ambassadors for Christ, God making his appeal through
us. We beseech you on behalf of Christ, be reconciled to God.
[2 Corinthians 5:20.]

Necessity is laid upon me. Woe to me if I do not preach the
gospel! [1 Corinthians 9:16.]

How are men to call upon him in whom they have not believed?
And how are they to believe in him of whom they have never
heard? And how are they to hear without a preacher? And how
can men preach unless they are sent? [Romans 10:14f.]

The whole collection breathes an atmosphere of willingness,
answerability and urgency. The whole impression is that of
men being driven along by the Holy Spirit with no other
consideration than to make Christ known.

We also know that they left churches behind them, not
merely converts, churches which, judging by the stuff of the
epistles, were well instructed. Perhaps the most telling charac-
teristic was that these groups were themselves self-propagating.
Paul could thank God that the church at Thessalonica had
not only withstood pressure and opposition, it had become a
sounding board for the gospel throughout the district, so that
when he arrived somewhere, people were telling him about
his earlier visits (1 Thessalonians 1:6–10). One of the secrets
of church growth in those days was simply that, although some
had been specially gifted to evangelize, the ordinary church
members were willing to share their faith and to suffer for
it. It has been said that the early church grew because they
were ready to gossip the gospel.

After all, they had something to talk about. Their experience
of Christ was not a nominal second-hand affair. It was a vital,
overflowing life-style which could not but attract those who
saw it. They had become, as Jesus had told them, the salt
of the earth and the light of the world (Matthew 5:13–16).

As he implied, it is the property of salt to taste and the property of light to shine. If they were what they professed to be, their influence would be inevitable. Paul uses a similar picture. They should be 'blameless and innocent, children of God without blemish in the midst of a crooked and perverse generation,' among whom they shone 'as lights in the world' (Philippians 2:15). They were a letter 'to be known and read by all men' (2 Corinthians 3:2).

It was a quality of life which stood out from the rest and which prompted people to ask questions. Peter tells his readers (1 Peter 4:15f.):

> Always be prepared to make a defence to any one who calls you to account for the hope that is in you, yet do it with gentleness and reverence; and keep your conscience clear, so that, when you are abused, those who revile your good behaviour in Christ may be put to shame.

The church proclaimed a life-changing gospel and there were changed lives to prove it. The world could respect and tolerate, or oppose and persecute, or give in and believe, and the evidence is that many in the first generation opted for the last course.

THE FUTURE OF THE CHURCH

Despite its long history, the story of the church is still incomplete. The work begun still goes on with the original principles being worked out to a greater or lesser degree, and it will do so until, as John foresaw, the Bridegroom will come for his Bride (Revelation 19:6–8):

> 'Hallelujah! For the Lord our God the Almighty reigns. Let us rejoice and exult and give him the glory, for the marriage of the Lamb has come, and his Bride has made herself ready; it was granted her to be clothed with fine linen, bright and pure' – for the fine linen is the righteous deeds of the saints.

God will complete the work which he has begun in his church here. In spite of their present imperfections and problems, God's people will be 'pure and blameless for the day of Christ, filled with the fruits of righteousness which come through Jesus Christ, to the glory and praise of God' (Philippians 1:10f.). 'When he appears we shall be like him,' says John, 'for we shall see him as he is.' (1 John 3:2.)

Jesus spoke about that great day when 'many will come from east and west and sit at table with Abraham, Isaac, and Jacob in the kingdom of heaven' (Matthew 8:11), 'a great multitude which no man could number, from every nation, from all tribes and peoples and tongues' (Revelation 7:9). The predictions and promises of both Old and New Testaments will be complete. The church will be what she was meant to be.

There are times when we can be depressed by what we see of the church as she is. We despair of ever seeing things change, but we have before us this double picture: we can look back and remember how the church began and all that God did for her in those early times, often in spite of the people themselves – and believe that he can do it again. And we can look forward to what the church will be in God's purpose – and remember that by the Holy Spirit we may have a foretaste of those blessings here and now. We ought to be able to look at the church and get a glimpse of heaven itself.

> You have come to mount Zion and to the city of the living God, the heavenly Jerusalem, and to innumerable angels in festal gathering, and to the assembly of the first-born who are enrolled in heaven, and to a judge who is God of all, and to the spirits of just men made perfect, and to Jesus.... [Hebrews 12:22–24.]

> Saviour, if of Zion's city
> I, through grace, a member am,
> Let the world deride or pity,
> I will glory in thy Name:
>
> Fading is the worldling's pleasure,
> All his boasted pomp and show;
> Solid joys and lasting treasure
> None but Zion's children know.

FURTHER READING

D. Bridge & D. Phypers, *The Water that Divides* (Inter-Varsity Press).

F. F. Bruce, *The Spreading Flame* (Paternoster Press).

M. Griffiths, *Cinderella with Amnesia* (Inter-Varsity Press).

G. E. Ladd, *A Theology of the New Testament* (Lutterworth Press).

H. Ridderbos, *Paul* (Eerdmans).

A. M. Stibbs, *God's Church* (Inter-Varsity Press).

J. R. W. Stott, *One People* (Falcon).

D. Watson, *I Believe in the Church* (Hodder & Stoughton).

INDEX